THE COURTSHIP
OF MILES STANDISH

THE
COURTSHIP
OF MILES
STANDISH

AND OTHER POEMS

BY
HENRY WADSWORTH LONGFELLOW

1858

WORDWELL
enterprises

CONTENTS

Introduction to The Courtship of Miles Standish   7

THE COURTSHIP OF MILES STANDISH

    I. Miles Standish   13
    II. Love and Friendship   19
    III. The Lover's Errand   25
    IV. John Alden   33
    V. The Sailing of the May Flower   39
    VI. Priscilla   45
    VII. The March of Miles Standish   49
    VIII. The Spinning-Wheel   55
    IX. The Wedding-Day   61

BIRDS OF PASSAGE   67

    Prometheus, or the Poet's Forethought   69
    The Ladder of St. Augustine   73
    The Phantom Ship   75
    The Warden of the Cinque Ports   77
    Haunted Houses   79
    In the Churchyard at Cambridge   81
    The Emperor's Bird's-Nest   83
    The Two Angels   85
    Daylight and Moonlight   87
    The Jewish Cemetery at Newport   89

Oliver Basselin   93
Victor Galbraith   97
My Lost Youth   99
The Ropewalk   103
The Golden Mile-Stone   107
Catawba Wine   109
Santa Filomena   113
The Discoverer of the North Cape   115
Daybreak   119
The Fiftieth Birthday of Agassiz   121
Children   123
Sandalphon   125
Epimetheus, or The Poet's Afterthought   127

Notes   131

ABOUT THE AUTHOR   135

INTRODUCTION

MILES STANDISH, born it has been conjectured about 1580, served as lieutenant in Queen Elizabeth's forces in the Netherlands, remained in or revisited that country in later years, became interested in the congregation of his countrymen at Leyden, and in their pastor, Robinson, and liking them and their principles, though he was not a member of their church, he joined the company who sailed in the Mayflower. He was not only the military leader, wise as well as valiant, of the Pilgrims, but filled more than one civil office of responsibility and trust. In 1630 he removed to Duxbury, so called from his ancestral home, and lived the remainder of his life in a house at the foot of Captain's Hill, whose name preserves the memory of his dwelling there. He died October 3, 1656, held in honor by all the colonists till the end of his days. That to the last he stoutly maintained his right to the great family inheritance which he believed should have been his, is shown in his will drawn up the year before his death, wherein he bequeaths those estates "surreptitiously detained from me" to his eldest son, as the lawful heir thereto.

When, in the cabin of the Mayflower, the Pilgrims set their hands to the compact by which they solemnly combined themselves "together into a civil body politic," one of the twelve signers — there were forty-one in all — who were entitled to have Mr. placed before their names, was William Mullins, whose surname, after a habit of the time, was variously spelled. On February 23, Bradford notes: "Die Mr. William White, Mr. William Mullins with two more. This month seventeen of our number die." Mr. Mullins, the father of Priscilla, is described as "a man pious and well-deserving, endowed with a considerable outward estate; and had it been the will of God that he had survived, might have proved a useful instrument in his place." In reading of the cruel hardships and sufferings of the devoted little band during that sad winter, it is some slight relief to know that it was a season of unusual mildness, —"such as was never seen here since," was declared in after years. Yet at its close the governor writes: "In three months past dies half our company; the greatest part in the depth of winter; the living scarce able to bury the dead; the well not sufficient to tend the sick, there being in their time of greatest distress, but six or seven, who spare no pains to help them." Two of the seven were Mr. Brewster, their reverend elder, and Miles Standish, their captain.

Early after the landing at the place selected for their habitation, they planned their village, —Fort Hill, where their cannon were to be placed, and from the foot of this hill "a fair street" running to the seashore. In this street, now called Leyden Street, but then First Street or simply The Street, only seven small dwellings, beside the Common House and storehouses, were erected during the first year. The houses their garden plots were close together, so that for safety they could "impale them round." The weaker members of the company must have remained on the Mayflower till the spring. The best description of New Plymouth, as it was then called, is that of Secretary de Rasières of the Dutch Colony, who visited it in 1627. After depicting the little town he says, "Upon the hill they have a large square house with a flat roof stayed with oak beams, upon the top of which they have six cannons, commanding the surrounding country. The lower part they use for their church, where they preach on Sundays and the usual holidays. They assemble by beat of drum, each with his musket or firelock, in front of the Captain's door; they have their cloaks on and place themselves in order three abreast, and are led by a sergeant without beat of drum. Behind comes the Governor in a long robe; beside him on the right hand comes the preacher, and on the left hand the Captain, and so they march in good order, and each sets his arms down near him. Thus they are constantly on their guard night and day." Life was ordered with dignity and decorum in that little community of God-fearing exiles on the verge of the wilderness; but as their numbers increased and dangers lessened, it is not wonderful that many longed for more spacious habitations outside the narrow town limits, and to the regret of the good Governor even some of the "first-comers sought wide farm lands in the country round, as did Standish, Alden, and others in founding Duxbury.

In reading the modest, unadorned narratives of the historians of that small company, so much more impressive than most of the eloquent tributes of later times, like Bradford one stands amazed at those poor people's condition." And as in simple, moving words he shows what that condition was, his closing sentences seem the only rightful ending: "Our fathers were Englishmen, which came over the ocean and were ready to perish in the wilderness. When they wandered in the wilderness and out of the way, and found no city to dwell in, both hungry and thirsty their soul was overwhelmed in them. But they cried unto the Lord, and he heard their voice, and looked on their adversity. Let them confess before the Lord his lovingkindness and his wonderful works before the children of men."

Longfellow, who through his mother was a descendant of John Alden, had at first intended to write a drama on the Courtship of Miles Standish, and in December, 1856, records that he had made some progress in it. But a year later he says: "I begin a new poem, Priscilla, to be a kind of Puritan pastoral. This I think will be a better treatment of the subject than the dramatic one. The poem will be an idyl of the Old Colony times, a bunch of mayflowers from the Plymouth woods. What it will turn out I do not know, but it gives me pleasure to write it, and that I count for something." This pleasure continued till the end; he worked steadily and rapidly, and the poem, now given its present title, was finished in March, 1858. Then came the inevitable reaction. "Printing Miles Standish and seeing all its defects as it stands before me in type. It is always disagreeable when the glow of composition is over to criticize what one has been in love with." But any doubt as to its reception was soon set at rest. The poem was published in the following October, and at once obtained a popularity, both in America and in England, which has proved enduring.

Scripture References.

THERE was one Book so familiar to even the humblest of the Pilgrims, that it became a part of themselves. It colored their ordinary thoughts, and often gave dignity and distinction to their common speech. But in moments of excitement, danger, distress, or any deep emotion, its supplications, its aspiration, its psalms of penitence or praise, its triumphant prophecies, seemed the natural expression of feeling to those who in the wilderness never lost the vision of the City of God which was the goal of their Pilgrimage. A real knowledge of the Bible was a general possession of their descendants, after the lapse of two centuries, and Longfellow uses it often, directly and indirectly, in his Old Colony poem, thus helping to give it the true atmosphere of the place and time.

Some words of John Alden (lines 32, 33) are an excellent illustration of the Puritan use of Biblical imagery. Standish (line 133) quotes almost verbally Genesis ii. 18. "No man having put his hand to the plough, and looking back, is fit for the kingdom of God" (S. Luke ix. 62) is used both in speech and in description (lines 245, 600). The burden of Psalm cxxxvi. (line 218) cheered the darkest days. Hebrew history and story are brought to mind in lines 361-364 (2 Samuel xi., xii. 1-14); 490 (2 Samuel xxiii.); 755 (1 Samuel xvii., Deuteronomy iii. 1-11); 936 (Ruth iv. 10, 11); 1013 (Numbers xiii. 23, 24); and 1015 (Genesis xxiv.). The departure of the children of Israel from Egypt, and their passage through the Red Sea (Exodus xiv.), are figuratively used in lines 376– 379; as are Revelation xix. 7 in line 388, Genesis ii. 10-14 in lines 664, 665, and Exodus xxx. 17-19 in line 931. Scriptural phraseology is used in lines 507 (Isaiah lii. 7) and 611 (Ephesians v. 18); while direct Scripture references or little changed quotations are found in 437 (S. Matthew vi. 4), 468 and 469 (Acts ii. 1-4), 613 and 820 (Acts xxviii. 15), 641 (2 Samuel xiv. 14), 834 (Hebrews xi. 34), and 917 (S. Matthew xix. 6). The praise of the virtuous woman, lines 857–864, is epitomized from Proverbs xxxi. 10-31.

It must be remembered in reading chronicles left by the Pilgrims, that Scriptural texts quoted by them are from the Genevan Bible, a translation made by exiles in Geneva in the reign of Queen Mary, and published in 1560. Many of the "first comers"[1] had left England before King James's Authorized Version was printed in 1611, and probably to the end of their lives they used the translation that had come to them from their fathers.

The Poem

This poem, like *Evangeline*, written in hexameters, has a lighter movement, due to the more playful character of the narrative. A slight change of accent in the first line prepares one for this livelier pace, and the reader will find that the lights and shades of the story use whatever elasticity there is in the hexameter, crisp, varying lines alternating with the steady pulse of the dactyl. The poet has built upon a slight tradition which has come down to us from the days of the Plymouth settlement, a story which depicts in a succession of scenes the life of the Old Colony. In doing this he has not cared to follow explicitly the succession of events, but has been true to the general history of the time, and has in each picture copied faithfully the essential characteristics of the original. He has taken the somewhat dry and unimaginative chronicles of the time, and touched them with a poetic light and warmth, and the reader of this poem who resumes such a book as Dr. Young's *Chronicles of the Pilgrims* will find the simple story of the early settlers to have gained in beauty.

---

1   Those that came in the Mayflower, the Fortune, and the Anne were in after years called the "first comers" or the "old comers," a distinction held in honor by all the colonists. Of the signers of the Compact, John Alden was the last survivor, dying in 1687, in bis eighty-ninth year.

I.

MILES STANDISH

In the Old Colony[1] days, in Plymouth the land of the Pilgrims,
To and fro in a room of his simple and primitive dwelling,[2]
Clad in doublet and hose, and boots of Cordovan[3] leather,
Strode, with a martial air, Miles Standish the Puritan Captain.
Buried in thought he seemed, with his hands behind him, and
      pausing
Ever and anon to behold his glittering weapons of warfare,
Hanging in shining array along the walls of the chamber, —
Cutlass and corslet[4] of steel, and his trusty sword of Damascus,
Curved at the point and inscribed with its mystical Arabic sentence,
While underneath, in a corner, were fowling piece,[5] musket, and
      matchlock.

1 The Old Colony is the name which has long been applied to that part of Massachusetts which was occupied by the Plymouth colonists whose first settlement
   was in 1620. Massachusetts Bay was the name by which was known the later
   collection of settlements made about Boston and Salem.
2 The first houses of the Pilgrims were of logs filled in with mortar and covered
   with thatch.
3 Cordova in Spain was celebrated for a preparation of goat-skin which took the
   name of Cordovan. Hence came cordwain, or Spanish tanned goat-skin, and in
   England shoemakers are still often called cordwainers. In France, too, the same
   word gave *cordonnier.*
4 The corslet was a light breastplate of armor. One of Standish's grandsons is
   said to have been in possession of his coat of mail. His sword is in the cabinet
   of the Massachusetts Historical Society. As "the identical sword-blade used by
   Miles Standish" is also in possession of the Pilgrim Society of Plymouth, the
   antiquary may take his choice between them, or credit Standish with a change
   of weapons, Damascus blades are swords or cimeters presenting upon their
   surface a variegated appearance of watering, as white, silvery, or black veins in
   fine lines and fillets. Such engraved blades were common in the East, and the
   most famous came from Damascus; the exact secret of the workmanship has
   never been fully discovered in the West.
5 A *fowling-piece* is a light gun for shooting birds; a *matchlock* was a musket, the
   lock of which held a match or piece of twisted rope prepared to retain fire. As

Short of stature he was, but strongly built and athletic,
Broad in the shoulders, deep-chested, with muscles and sinews
    of iron;
Brown as a nut was his face, but his russet beard was already
Flaked with patches of snow, as hedges some times in November.
Near him was seated John Alden, his friend, and household
    companion,[6]
Writing with diligent speed at a table of pine by the window;
Fair-haired, azure-eyed, with delicate Saxon complexion,
Having the dew of his youth, and the beauty thereof, as the captives
Whom Saint Gregory saw, and exclaimed,"Not Angles but Angels."[7]
Youngest of all was he of the men who came in the May Flower.

Suddenly breaking the silence, the diligent scribe interrupting,

---

late as 1687 matchlocks were used instead of flint-locks, which had then come into general use. In Bradford and Winslow's Journal (Young's *Chronicles of the Pilgrims*, p. 125), we are told of a party setting out "with every man his musket, sword, and corselet, under the conduct of Captain Miles Standish." That these muskets were matchlocks, appears from another passage in the same journal (p. 142) : "Then we lighted all our matches and prepared our selves, concluding that we were near their dwellings."

6   Bradford, the historian of the Plymouth Plantation, says that John Alden, who was one of the Mayflower company, hired for a cooper at Southampton, where the ship victualed; and being a hopeful young man, was much desired, but left to his own liking to go or stay when he came here [to Plymouth, that is: but he stayed and married here." In this picture of Miles Stan dish and John Alden, some have professed to see a miniature likeness to Oliver Cromwell and John Milton.

7   The story of the first mission to heathen England is referred to here. A monk named Gregory, in the sixth century, passed through the slave-market at Rome, and there amongst other captives he saw three fair-complexioned and fair-haired boys, in striking contrast to the dusky captives about them. He asked whence they came, and was answered,"From Britain," and that they were called *Angli,* which was the Latin form of the name by which they called them-selves, and from which Anglo, England, and English are derived. " *Non Angli sed Angeli,*" replied Gregory; "they have the face of angels, not of Angles, and they ought to be fellow heirs of heaven." Years afterward, the story runs, when Gregory was pope, he remembered the fair captives, and sent St. Augustine to carry Christianity to them. The story will be found at length in E. A. Freeman's *Old English History for Children,* p. 44.

Spake, in the pride of his heart, Miles Standish the Captain of
    Plymouth.
"Look at these arms," he said, "the warlike weapons that hang here
Burnished and bright and clean, as if for parade or inspection!
This is the sword of Damascus I fought with in Flanders;[8] this
    breastplate,
Well I remember the day! once saved my life in a skirmish;
Here in front you can see the very dint of the bullet
Fired point-blank at my heart by a Spanish arcabucero.[9]
Had it not been of sheer steel, the forgotten bones of Miles Standish
Would at this moment be mould, in their grave in the Flemish
    morasses."
Thereupon answered John Alden, but looked not up from his
    writing:
"Truly the breath of the Lord hath slackened the speed of the bullet;
He in his mercy preserved you, to be our shield and our weapon!"
Still the Captain continued, unheeding the words of the stripling:
"See, how bright they are burnished, as if in an arsenal hanging;
That is because I have done it myself, and not left it to others.
Serve yourself, would you be well served, is an excellent adage;
So I take care of my arms, as you of your pens and your inkhorn.[10]
Then, too, there are my soldiers, my great, invincible army,[11]
Twelve men, all equipped, having each his rest and his matchlock,
Eighteen shillings a month, together with diet and pillage,
And, like Cæsar, I know the name of each of my soldiers!"
This he said with a smile, that danced in his eyes, as the sunbeams

---

8   The history of Miles Standish is not clearly known, but he was a soldier in the
    Low Countries during the defence of the Netherlands against the Spanish pow-
    er, and the poet has made much of this little knowledge that we have.
9   *Arcabucero* is Spanish for archer, and the same term passed over, as weapons
    changed, into a musketeer and gunsmith.
10 There is some uncertainty about the derivation of the word *mkhorn*. The usual
    interpretation refers to the custom of scribes carrying ink in a horn attached
    to their dress, but some etymologists make it a corruption from *inkern,* the ter-
    minations *erne* and *eron* coming from the Saxon *ern, earn,* a secret place to put
    anything in, *inkern* being thus a little vessel into which we put ink.
11 The formation of the military company was due chiefly to the serious losses
    that befell the Pilgrims during the first winter, leading them to make careful
    provision against surprises and attacks from the Indians.

Dance on the waves of the sea, and vanish again in a moment.
Alden laughed as he wrote, and still the Captain continued:
Look! you can see from this window my brazen howitzer planted
High on the roof of the church, a preacher who speaks to the
     purpose,[12]
Steady, straight-forward, and strong, with irresistible logic,
Orthodox, flashing conviction right into the hearts of the heathen.
Now we are ready, I think, for any assault of the Indians;
Let them come, if they like, and the sooner they try it the better,—
Let them come if they like, be it sagamore, sachem, or pow-wow,[13]
Aspinet, Samoset, Corbitant, Squanto, or Tokamahamon!"[14]

Long at the window he stood, and wistfully gazed on the
     landscape,
Washed with a cold gray mist, the vapory breath of the east-wind,
Forest and meadow and hill, and the steel blue rim of the ocean,
Lying silent and sad, in the afternoon shadows and sunshine.
Over his countenance flitted a shadow like those on the landscape,
Gloom intermingled with light; and his voice was subdued with
     emotion,
Tenderness, pity, regret, as after a pause he proceeded:
"Yonder there, on the hill by the sea, lies buried Rose Standish;
Beautiful rose of love, that bloomed for me by the wayside!
She was the first to die of all who came in the May Flower!
Green above her is growing the field of wheat we have sown there,[15]
Better to hide from the Indian scouts the graves of our people,

---

12 One of the earliest structures raised by the Pilgrims was a platform upon the
    hill overlooking the settlement, where they mounted five guns. They had also
    a common house for rendezvous, twenty feet square, but the planting of guns
    upon the log-built meeting-house belongs to a later date.
13 The *sagamore* was an Indian chief of the subordinate class; the *sachem* a princi-
    pal chief; the *pow-wow* a medicine man or conjurer.
14 Names of Indians who are mentioned in the early chronicles.
15 The dead were buried on a bluff by the water-side during that first terrible
    winter, and the marks of burial were carefully effaced, lest the Indians should
    discover how the colony had been weakened. The tradition is preserved in
    Holmes's *Annals*.

THE COURTSHIP OF MILES STANDISH

Lest they should count them and see how many already have
    perished!"
Sadly his face he averted, and strode up and down, and was
    thoughtful.

Fixed to the opposite wall was a shelf of books, and among them
Prominent three, distinguished alike for bulk and for binding;
Bariffe's Artillery Guide, and the Commentaries of Cæsar,[16]
Out of the Latin translated by Arthur Goldinge of London,[17]
And, as if guarded by these, between them was standing the Bible.
Musing a moment before them, Miles Standish paused, as if
    doubtful
Which of the three he should choose for his consolation and
    comfort,
Whether the wars of the Hebrews, the famous campaigns of the
    Romans,
Or the Artillery practice, designed for belligerent Christians.
Finally down from its shelf he dragged the ponderous Roman,
Seated himself at the window, and opened the book, and in silence
Turned o'er the well-worn leaves, where thumb marks thick on
    the margin,
Like the trample of feet, proclaimed the battle was hottest.
Nothing was heard in the room but the hurrying pen of the
    stripling,
Busily writing epistles important, to go by the May Flower,[18]

---

16 The elaborate title of Standish's military book was: "Militarie Discipline : or the
Young Artillery Man, Wherein is Discoursed and Shown the Postures both of
Musket and Pike, the Exactest way, &c., Together with the Exercise of the Foot
in their Motions, with much variety : As also, diverse and several Forms for
the Imbatteling small or great Bodies demonstrated by the number of a single
Company with their Reducements. Very necessary for all such as are Studious
in the Art Military. Whereunto is also added the Postures and Beneficiall Use of
the Halfe-Pike joyned with the Musket. With the way to draw up the Swedish
Brigade. By Colonel William Barriffe." Barriffe was a Puritan, and added to his
title-page: "Psalmes 144: 1. Blessed be the Lord my Strength which teacheth my
hands to warre and my fingers to fight."
17 Goldinge was a voluminous translator, and his translation of Ovid's *Metamor-
phoses* was highly regarded. He was patronized by Sir Philip Sidney.
18 The Mayflower began her return voyage April 5, 1621. Not a single one of the

Ready to sail on the morrow, or next day at latest, God willing!
Homeward bound with the tidings of all that terrible winter,
Letters written by Alden, and full of the name of Priscilla,[19]
Full of the name and the fame of the Puritan maiden Priscilla!

emigrants returned in her, in spite of the "terrible winter."
19 Among the names of the Mayflower company are those of Mr. William
Mullines and his wife, and 2 children, Joseph and Priscilla; and a servant, Robert Carter."

II.

LOVE AND FRIENDSHIP

NOTHING was heard in the room but the hurrying pen of the
    stripling,
Or an occasional sigh from the laboring heart of the Captain,
Reading the marvellous words and achievements of Julius Cæsar.
After a while he exclaimed, as he smote with his hand, palm
    downwards,
Heavily on the page: "A wonderful man was this Cæsar!
You are a writer, and I am a fighter, but here is a fellow
Who could both write and fight, and in both was equally skilful!"
Straightway answered and spake John Alden, the comely, the
    youthful:
"Yes, he was equally skilled, as you say, with his pen and his
    weapons.
Somewhere have I read, but where I forget, he could dictate
Seven letters at once, at the same time writing his memoirs.
"Truly," continued the Captain, not heeding or hearing the other,
"Truly a wonderful man was Caius Julius Cæsar!
Better be first, he said, in a little Iberian village,[1]
Than be second in Rome, and I think he was right when he said it.
Twice was he married before he was twenty, and many times after;
Battles five hundred he fought, and a thousand cities he conquered;
He, too, fought in Flanders, as he himself has recorded;
Finally he was stabbed by his friend, the orator Brutus!
Now, do you know what he did on a certain occasion in Flanders,

---

1 "In his journey, as he was crossing the Alps and passing by a small village of
the barbarians with but few inhabitants, and those wretchedly poor, his companions asked the question among themselves by way of mockery if there were
any canvassing for offices there ; any contention which should be uppermost,
or feuds of great men one against another. To which Cæsar made answer seri-
ously, 'For my part I had rather be the first man among these fellows, than the
second man in Rome.'" Plutarch's *Life of Cæsar*, A. H. Clough's translation.

When the rear-guard of his army retreated, the front giving way
    too,
And the immortal Twelfth Legion was crowded so closely together
There was no room for their swords? Why, he seized a shield from
    a soldier,
Put himself straight at the head of his troops, and commanded
    the captains,
Calling on each by his name, to order forward the ensigns;
Then to widen the ranks, and give more room for their weapons;
So he won the day, the battle of something-or other.[2]
That's what I always say; if you wish a thing to be well done,
You must do it yourself, you must not leave it to others!"

All was silent again; the Captain continued his reading
Nothing was heard in the room but the hurrying pen of the stripling
Writing epistles important to go next day by the May Flower,
Filled with the name and the fame of the Puritan maiden Priscilla;
Every sentence began or closed with the name of Priscilla,
'Till the treacherous pen, to which he confided the secret,
Strove to betray it by singing and shouting the name of Priscilla!
Finally closing his book, with a bang of the ponderous cover,
Sudden and loud as the sound of a soldier grounding his musket,
Thus to the young man spake Miles Standish the Captain of
    Plymouth:
"When you have finished your work, I have something important
    to tell you.
Be not however in haste; I can wait; I shall not be impatient!"
Straightway Alden replied, as he folded the last of his letters,
Pushing his papers aside, and giving respectful attention:
"Speak; for whenever you speak, I am always ready to listen,
Always ready to hear whatever pertains to Miles Standish."
Thereupon answered the Captain, embarrassed, and culling his
    phrases:
"'Tis not good for a man to be alone, say the Scriptures.
This I have said before, and again and again I repeat it;

---

2   The account of this battle will be found in *Cæsar's Commentaries*, book II. ch. 10.

Every hour in the day, I think it, and feel it, and say it.
Since Rose Standish died, my life has been weary and dreary;
Sick at heart have I been, beyond the healing of friendship
Oft in my lonely hours have I thought of the maiden Priscilla.
She is alone in the world; her father and mother and brother
Died in the winter together;[3] I saw her going and coming,
Now to the grave of the dead, and now to the bed of the dying,
Patient, courageous, and strong, and said to myself, that if ever
There were angels on earth, as there are angels in heaven,
Two have I seen and known; and the angel whose name is Priscilla
Holds in my desolate life the place which the other abandoned.
Long have I cherished the thought, but never have dared to reveal it,
Being a coward in this, though valiant enough for the most part
Go to the damsel Priscilla, the loveliest maiden of Plymouth,
Say that a blunt old Captain, a man not of words but of actions,
Offers his hand and his heart, the hand and heart of a soldier.
Not in these words, you know, but this in short is my meaning;
I am a maker of war, and not a maker of phrases.
You, who are bred as a scholar, can say it in elegant language,
Such as you read in your books of the pleadings and wooings of
        lovers,
Such as you think best adapted to win the heart of a maiden."

    When he had spoken, John Alden, the fair haired, taciturn
        stripling,
All aghast at his words, surprised, embarrassed, bewildered,
Trying to mask his dismay by treating the subject with lightness,\
Trying to smile, and yet feeling his heart stand still in his bosom,
Just as a timepiece stops in a house that is stricken by lightning,
Thus made answer and spake, or rather stammered than answered:
"Such a message as that, I am sure I should mangle and mar it;
If you would have it well done, —I am only repeating your maxim,—
You must do it yourself, you must not leave it to others!"

3 "Mr. Molines, and his wife, his sone and his servant, dyed the first winter.
   Only his daughter Priscila survived and married with John Alden, who are
   both living and have 11 children." Bradford's *History of Plymouth Plantation*, p.
   452.

But with the air of a man whom nothing can turn from his purpose,
Gravely shaking his head, made answer the Captain of Plymouth:
"Truly the maxim is good, and I do not mean to gainsay it;
But we must use it discreetly, and not waste powder for nothing.
Now, as I said before, I was never a maker of phrases.
I can march up to a fortress and summon the place to surrender,
But march up to a woman with such a proposal, I dare not.
I'm not afraid of bullets, nor shot from the mouth of a cannon,
But of a thundering "No!" point-blank from the mouth of a woman,
 That I confess I'm afraid of, nor am I ashamed to confess it!
So you must grant my request, for you are an elegant scholar,
Having the graces of speech, and skill in the turning of phrases."
Taking the hand of his friend, who still was reluctant and doubtful,
Holding it long in his own, and pressing it kindly, he added:
"Though I have spoken thus lightly, yet deep is the feeling that
         prompts me;
Surely you cannot refuse what I ask in the name of our friendship!"
Then made answer John Alden: "The name of friendship is sacred;
What you demand in that name, I have not the power to deny you!"
So the strong will prevailed, subduing and moulding the gentler,
Friendship prevailed over love, and Alden went on his errand.

SURELY YOU CANNOT REFUSE

III.

THE LOVER'S ERRAND

So the strong will prevailed, and Alden went on his errand,
Out of the street of the village, and into the paths of the forest,
Into the tranquil woods, where blue-birds and robins were building
Towns in the populous trees, with hanging gardens of verdure,[1]
Peaceful, aerial cities of joy and affection and freedom.
All around him was calm, but within him commotion and conflict,
Love contending with friendship, and self with each generous
      impulse.
To and fro in his breast his thoughts were heaving and dashing,
As in a foundering ship, with every roll of the vessel,
Washes the bitter sea, the merciless surge of the ocean!
"Must I relinquish it all," he cried with a wild lamentation,
"Must I relinquish it all, the joy, the hope, the illusion?
Was it for this I have loved, and waited, and worshipped in silence?
Was it for this I have followed the flying feet and the shadow
Over the wintry sea, to the desolate shores of New England?
Truly the heart is deceitful, and out of its depths of corruption
Rise, like an exhalation, the misty phantoms of passion;
Angels of light they seem, but are only delusions of Satan.
All is clear to me now; I feel it, I see it distinctly!
This is the hand of the Lord; it is laid upon me in anger,
For I have followed too much the heart's desires and devices,
Worshipping Astaroth blindly, and impious idols of Baal.[2]
This is the cross I must bear; the sin and the swift retribution."

So through the Plymouth woods John Alden went on his errand;

---

1 Compare the *populous nests* in Evangeline, 1. 136. In the *hanging gardens of verdure* there is reference to the famous hanging gardens of Babylon.
2 *Astaroth*, in the Old Testament Scripture, is the form used for the principal female divinity, as *Baal* of the principal male divinity of the Phoenicians.

Crossing the brook at the ford, where it brawled over pebble and
    shallow,
Gathering still, as he went, the May-flowers blooming around him,[3]
Fragrant, filling the air with a strange and wonderful sweetness,
Children lost in the woods, and covered with,leaves in their
    slumber.
"Puritan flowers," he said, "and the type of Puritan maidens,
Modest and simple and sweet, the very type of Priscilla!
So I will take them to her; to Priscilla the May-flower of Plymouth,
Modest and simple and sweet, as a parting gift will I take them;
Breathing their silent farewells, as they fade and wither and perish,
Soon to be thrown away as is the heart of the giver."
So through the Plymouth woods John Alden went on his errand;
Came to an open space, and saw the disk of the ocean,
Sailless, sombre and cold with the comfortless breath of the
    east-wind;
Saw the new-built house, and people at work in a meadow;
Heard, as he drew near the door, the musical voice of Priscilla
Singing the hundredth Psalm, the grand old Puritan anthem,[4]
Music that Luther sang to the sacred words of the Psalmist,
Full of the breath of the Lord, consoling and comforting many.
Then, as he opened the door, he beheld the form of the maiden

---

3 The *Mayflower* is the well-known *Epigæa repens*, sometimes also called the Trailing Arbutus. The name *Mayflower* was familiar in England, as the application
of it to the historic ship shows, but it was applied by the English, and is still, to
the hawthorn. Its use here in connection with *Epigæa repens* dates from a very
early day, some claiming that the first Pilgrims used it, in affectionate memory
of the vessel and its English flower associations.

4 The words in the version which Priscilla used sound some what rude to
modern ears, but the music is substantially what we know as Old Hundred.
The poet tells us (1. 231) that it was Ainsworth's translation which she used.
Ainsworth became a Brownist in 1590, suffered persecution, and found refuge
in Holland, where he published learned commentaries and translations His
version of Psalm c. is as follows: "1. Bow to Jehovah all the earth. 2. Serve ye
Jehovah with gladness; before him come with singing mirth. % Know that
Jehovah he God is. It's be that made us and not we, his flock and sheep of his
feeding. 4. Oh, with confession enter ye his gates, his courtyard with praising.
Confess to him, bless ye his name. 5. Because Jehovah he good is ; his mercy
ever is the same, and his faith unto all ages."

Seated beside her wheel, and the carded wool like a snow-drift
Piled at her knee, her white hands feeding the ravenous spindle,
While with her foot on the treadle she guided the wheel in its
    motion.
Open wide on her lap lay the well-worn psalm book of Ainsworth,
Printed in Amsterdam, the words and the music together,
Rough-hewn, angular notes, like stones in the wall of a churchyard,
Darkened and overhung by the running vine of the verses.
Such was the book from whose pages she sang the old Puritan
    anthem,
She, the Puritan girl, in the solitude of the forest,
Making the humble house and the modest apparel of home-spun
Beautiful with her beauty, and rich with the wealth of her being!
Over him rushed, like a wind that is keen and cold and relentless,
Thoughts of what might have been, and the weight and woe of
    his errand;
All the dreams that had faded, and all the hopes that had vanished,
All his life henceforth a dreary and tenantless mansion,
Haunted by vain regrets, and pallid, sorrowful faces.
Still he said to himself, and almost fiercely he said it,
"Let not him that putteth his hand to the plough look backwards;
Though the ploughshare cut through the flowers of life to its
    fountains,
Though it pass o'er the graves of the dead and the hearths of the
    living,
It is the will of the Lord; and his mercy endureth for ever!"

   So he entered the house: and the hum of the wheel and the singing
Suddenly ceased; for Priscilla, aroused by his step on the threshold,
Rose as he entered, and gave him her hand, in signal of welcome,
Saying, "I knew it was you, when I heard your step in the passage;
For I was thinking of you, as I sat there singing and spinning."
Awkward and dumb with delight, that a thought of him had been
    mingled
Thus in the sacred psalm, that came from the heart of the maiden.
Silent before her he stood, and gave her the flowers for an answer,

HENRY WADSWORTH LONGFELLOW

Finding no words for his thought. He remembered that day in
     the winter,
After the first great snow, when he broke a path from the village,
Reeling and plunging along through the drifts that encumbered
     the doorway,
Stamping the snow from his feet as he entered the house, and
     Priscilla
Laughed at his snowy locks, and gave him a seat by the fireside,
Grateful and pleased to know he had thought of her in the
     snow-storm.
Had he but spoken then! perhaps not in vain had he spoken;
Now it was all too late; the golden moment had vanished!
So he stood there abashed, and gave her the Flowers for an answer.

   Then they sat down and talked of the birds and the beautiful
     Spring-time,
Talked of their friends at home, and the May Flower that sailed
     on the morrow.
"I have been thinking all day," said gently the Puritan maiden,
"Dreaming all night, and thinking all day, of the hedge-rows of
     England,—
They are in blossom now, and the country is all like a garden;
Thinking of lanes and fields, and the song of the lark and the linnet,
Seeing the village street, and familiar faces of neighbors
Going about as of old, and stopping to gossip together,
And, at the end of the street, the village church, with the ivy
Climbing the old gray tower, and the quiet graves in the churchyard.
Kind are the people I live with, and dear to me my religion;
Still my heart is so sad, that I wish myself back in Old England.
You will say it is wrong, but I cannot help it:
I almost wish myself back in Old England, I feel so lonely and
     wretched."

   Thereupon answered the youth: —"Indeed, I do not condemn you;
Stouter hearts than a woman's have quailed in this terrible winter.
Yours is tender and trusting, and needs a stronger to lean on;

So I have come to you now, with an offer and proffer of marriage
Made by a good man and true, Miles Standish the Captain of
    Plymouth!"

  Thus he delivered his message, the dexterous writer of letters,
Did not embellish the theme, nor array it in beautiful phrases,
But came straight to the point, and blurted it out like a schoolboy;
Even the Captain himself could hardly have said it more bluntly.
Mute with amazement and sorrow, Priscilla the Puritan maiden
Looked into Alden's face, her eyes dilated with wonder,
Feeling his words like a blow, that stunned her and rendered her
    speechless;
Till at length she exclaimed, interrupting the ominous silence:"
If the great Captain of Plymouth is so very eager to wed me,
Why does he not come himself, and take the trouble to woo me?
If I am not worth the wooing, I surely am not worth the winningı"
Then John Alden began explaining and smoothing the matter,
Making it worse as he went, by saying the Captain was busy,—
Had no time for such things; — such things! the words grating
    harshly
Fell on the ear of Priscilla; and swift as a flash she made answer:
"Has he no time for such things, as you call it, before he is married,
Would he be likely to find it, or make it, after the wedding?
That is the way with you men; you don't understand us, you cannot.
When you have made up your minds, after thinking of this one
    and that one,
Choosing, selecting, rejecting, comparing one with another,
Then you make known your desire, with abrupt and sudden avowal,
And are offended and hurt, and indignant perhaps, that a woman
Does not respond at once to a love that she never suspected,
Does not attain at a bound the height to which you have been
    climbing.
This is not right nor just: for surely a woman's affection
Is not a thing to be asked for, and had for only the asking
When one is truly in love, one not only says it, but shows it.
Had he but waited awhile, had he only showed that he loved me,

Even this Captain of yours —who knows? at last might have won me,
Old and rough as he is; but now it never can happen."

Still John Alden went on, unheeding the words of Priscilla,
Urging the suit of his friend, explaining, persuading, expanding;
Spoke of his courage and skill, and of all his battles in Flanders,
How with the people of God he had chosen to suffer affliction,
How, in return for his zeal, they had made him Captain of Plymouth;
He was a gentleman born, could trace his pedigree plainly
Back to Hugh Standish of Duxbury Hall, in Lancashire, England,[5]
Who was the son of Ralph, and the grandson of Thurston de
    Standish;
Heir unto vast estates, of which he was basely defrauded,
Still bore the family arms, and had for his crest a cock argent
Combed and wattled gules, and all the rest of the blazon.[6]
He was a man of honor, of noble and generous nature;
Though he was rough, he was kindly; she knew how during the
    winter
He had attended the sick, with a hand as gentle as woman's;
Somewhat hasty and hot, he could not deny it,and headstrong,
Stern as a soldier might be, but hearty, and placable always,
Not to be laughed at and scorned, because he was little of stature,
For he was great of heart, magnanimous, courtly, courageous;

---

5 "There are at this time in England two ancient families of the name, one of
    Standish Hall, and the other of Duxbury Park, both in Lancashire, who trace
    their descent from a common ancestor, Ralph de Standish, living in 1221. There
    seems always to have been a military spirit in the family. Froissart, relating
    in his Chronicles the memorable meeting between Richard II. and Wat Tyler,
    says that after the rebel was struck from his horse by William Walworth, then
    a squyer of the kynges alyted, called John Standysshe, and he drewe out his
    sworde, and put into Wat Tyler's belye, and so he dyed. For this act Standish
    was knighted. In 1415 another Sir John Standish fought at the battle of Ag-
    incourt. From his giving the name of Duxbury to the town where he settled,
    near Plymouth, and calling his eldest son Alexander (a common name in the
    Standish family), I have no doubt that Miles was a scion from this ancient and
    warlike stock." Young's *Chronicles of the Pilgrims*, footnote, p. 125.
6 Terms of heraldry. *Argent* is silver and gules red.

PRISCILLA

Any woman in Plymouth, nay, any woman in England,
Might be happy and proud to be called the wife of Miles Standish!

But as he warmed and glowed, in his simple and eloquent
language,
Quite forgetful of self, and full of the praise of his rival,
Archly the maiden smiled, and, with eyes over running with
laughter,
Said, in a tremulous voice, "Why don't you speak for yourself,
John?"

IV.

JOHN ALDEN

Into the open air John Alden, perplexed and bewildered,
Rushed like a man insane, and wandered alone by the sea-side;
Paced up and down the sands, and bared his head to the east-wind,
Cooling his heated brow, and the fire and fever within him.
Slowly as out of the heavens, with apocalyptical splendors,
Sank the City of God, in the vision of John the Apostle,[1]
So, with its cloudy walls of chrysolite, jasper, and sapphire,
Sank the broad red sun, and over its turrets uplifted
Glimmered the golden reed of the angel who measured the city.

"Welcome, O wind of the East!" he exclaimed in his wild
    exultation,
"Welcome, o wind of the East, from the caves of the misty Atlantic!
Blowing o'er fields of dulse, and measureless meadows of sea-grass,
Blowing o'er rocky wastes, and the grottos and gardens of ocean!
Lay thy cold, moist hand on my burning forehead, and wrap me
Close in thy garments of mist, to allay the fever within me!"

Like an awakened conscience, the sea was moaning and tossing,
Beating remorseful and loud the mutable sands of the sea-shore.
Fierce in his soul was the struggle and tumult of passions
    contending;
Love triumphant and crowned, and friendship wounded and
    bleeding,
Passionate cries of desire, and importunate pleadings of duty!
"Is it my fault," he said, "that the maiden has chosen between us?
Is it my fault that he failed, —my fault that I am the victor?"

---

1 See the last chapter of the Book of Revelation.

Then within him there thundered a voice, like the voice of the
    Prophet:
"It hath displeased the Lord!" —and he thought of David's
    transgression,
Bathsheba's beautiful face, and his friend in the front of the battle!
Shame and confusion of guilt, and abasement and self-condemnation,
Overwhelmed him at once; and he cried in the deepest contrition:
"It hath displeased the Lord! It is the temptation of Satan!"

   Then, uplifting his head, he looked at the sea, and beheld there
Dimly the shadowy form of the May Flower riding at anchor,
Rocked on the rising tide, and ready to sail on the morrow;
Heard the voices of men through the mist, the rattle of cordage
Thrown on the deck, the shouts of the mate, and the sailors'
    "Ay, ay, Sir!"
Clear and distinct, but not loud, in the dripping air of the twilight.
Still for a moment he stood, and listened, and stared at the vessel,
Then went hurriedly on, as one who, seeing a phantom,
Stops, then quickens his pace, and follows the beckoning shadow.
"Yes, it is plain to me now," he murmured; "the hand of the Lord is
Leading me out of the land of darkness, the bondage of error,
Through the sea, that shall lift the walls of its waters around me,
Hiding me, cutting me off, from the cruel thoughts that pursue me.
Back will I go o'er the ocean, this dreary land will abandon,
Her whom I may not love, and him whom my heart has offended.
Better to be in my grave in the green old churchyard in England,
Close by my mother's side, and among the dust of my kindred;
Better be dead and forgotten, than living in shame and dishonor!
Sacred and safe and unseen, in the dark of the narrow chamber
With me my secret shall lie, like a buried jewel that glimmers
Bright on the hand that is dust, in the chambers of silence and
    darkness,—
Yes, as the marriage ring of the great espousal hereafter!"

   Thus as he spake, he turned, in the strength of his strong
    resolution,

Leaving behind him the shore, and hurried along in the twilight,
Through the congenial gloom of the forest silent and sombre,
Till he beheld the lights in the seven houses of Plymouth,[2]
Shining like seven stars in the dusk and mist of the evening.
Soon he entered his door, and found the redoubtable Captain
Sitting alone, and absorbed in the martial pages of Cæsar,
Fighting some great campaign in Hainault or Brabant or Flanders.
"Long have you been on your errand," he said with a cheery
 demeanor,
Even as one who is waiting an answer, and fears not the issue.
"Not far off is the house, although the woods are between us;
But you have lingered so long, that while you were going and
 coming
I have fought ten battles and sacked and demolished a city.
Come, sit down, and in order relate to me all that has happened."

 Then John Alden spake, and related the wondrous adventure,
From beginning to end, minutely, just as it happened;
How he had seen Priscilla, and how he had sped in his courtship,
Only smoothing a little, and softening down her refusal.
But when he came at length to the words Priscilla had spoken,
Words so tender and cruel: "Why don't you speak for yourself,
 John?"
Up leaped the Captain of Plymouth, and stamped on the floor,
 till his armor
Clanged on the wall, where it hung, with a sound of sinister omen.
All his pent-up wrath burst forth in a sudden explosion,
Even as a hand-grenade, that scatters destruction around i.
Wildly he shouted, and loud: "John Alden! you have betrayed me!
Me, Miles Standish, your friend! have supplanted, defrauded,
 betrayed me!
One of my ancestors ran his sword through the heart of Wat Tyler;

2 In a letter written by Edward Winslow, December 11, 1621, to a friend in
 England, he says : "You shall understand that in this little time that a few of us
 have been here, we have built seven dwelling-houses and four for the use of
 the plantation." Young's *Chronicles*, p. 230.

Who shall prevent me from running my own through the heart
    of a traitor?
Yours is the greater treason, for yours is a treason to friendship!
You, who lived under my roof, whom I cherished and loved as a
    brother;
You, who have fed at my board, and drunk at my cup, to whose
    keeping
I have intrusted my honor, my thoughts the most sacred and
    secret,—
You too, Brutus! ah woe to the name of friendship hereafter!
Brutus was Cæsar's friend, and you were mine, but henceforward
Let there be nothing between us save war, and implacable hatred!"

So spake the Captain of Plymouth, and strode about in the
    chamber,
Chafing and choking with rage ; like cords were the veins on his
    temples.
But in the midst of his anger a man appeared at the doorway,
Bringing in uttermost haste a message of urgent importance,
Rumors of danger and war and hostile incursions of Indians!
Straightway the Captain paused, and, without further question
    or parley,
Took from the nail on the wall his sword with its scabbard of iron,
Buckled the belt round his waist, and, frowning fiercely, departed.
Alden was left alone. He heard the clank of the scabbard
Growing fainter and fainter, and dying away in the distance.
Then he arose from his seat, and looked forth into the darkness,
Felt the cool air blow on his cheek, that was hot with the insult,
Lifted his eyes to the heavens, and, folding his hands as in
    childhood,
Prayed in the silence of night to the Father who seeth in secret.

Meanwhile the choleric Captain strode wrathful away to the
    council,
Found it already assembled, impatiently waiting his coming;
Men in the middle of life, austere and grave in deportment,

Only one of them old, the hill that was nearest to heaven,
Covered with snow, but erect, the excellent Elder of Plymouth.[3]
God had sifted three kingdoms to find the wheat for this planting,[4]
Then had sifted the wheat, as the living seed of a nation;
So say the chronicles old, and such is the faith of the people!
Near them was standing an Indian, in attitude stern and defiant,
Naked down to the waist, and grim and ferocious in aspect;
While on the table before them was lying unopened a Bible,
Ponderous, bound in leather, brass-studded, printed in Holland,[5]
And beside it outstretched the skin of a rattlesnake glittered,[6]
Filled, like a quiver, with arrows; a signal and challenge of warfare,
Brought by the Indian, and speaking with arrowy tongues of
    defiance.
This Miles Standish beheld, as he entered, and heard them debating
What were an answer befitting the hostile message and menace,
Talking of this and of that, contriving, suggesting, objecting;
One voice only for peace, and that the voice of the Elder,

---

3   Elder William Brewster. The elder of the Pilgrim Church was the minister who
taught and administered the sacraments. He was assisted also by an officer
named the ruling elder, whose function was much the same as that of the dea-
con in Congregational churches at the present day. The teaching elder included
ruling among his duties; the ruling elder sometimes taught in the absence of
his superior; the teaching elder was maintained by the people; the ruling elder
was not withdrawn from other occupations, and maintained himself. Brewster
was the ruling elder in the little Plymouth Church, but in the absence of Robinson was also their teacher.

4   In Stoughton's election sermon of 1668 occurs the first use, apparently, of this
oft-quoted phrase: "God sifted a whole nation that he might send a choice
grain over into this wilderness."

5   The Genevan Bible was the favorite version of the Puritans, and was clung
to long after the King James version had been issued. Owing to obstacles in
England, the Bible was frequently printed on the Continent, once at any rate at
Amsterdam.

6   As a matter of history, the first recorded instance of the rattlesnake skin challenge was in January, 1622, when Tisquantum the Indian brought a defiance
from Canonicus, and the governor returned the skin stuffed with bullets.
Holmes, in his *Annals* (i. 177), reminds the reader: "There is a remarkable co-
incidence in the form of this challenge given by the Scythian prince to Darius.
Five arrows made a part of the present sent by his herald to the Persian king.
The manner of declaring war by the Aracaunian Indians of South America was
by sending from town to town an arrow clinched in a dead man's hand."

Judging it wise and well that some at least were converted,[7]
Rather than any were slain, for this was but Christian behavior!
Then outspake Miles Standish, the stalwart Captain of Plymouth,
Muttering deep in his throat, for his voice was husky with anger,
"What! do you mean to make war with milk and the water of roses?
Is it to shoot red squirrels you have your howitzer planted
There on the roof of the church, or is it to shoot red devils?
Truly the only tongue that is understood by a savage
Must be the tongue of fire that speaks from the mouth of the
    cannon!"
Thereupon answered and said the excellent Elder of Plymouth,
Somewhat amazed and alarmed at this irreverent language:
"Not so thought Saint Paul, nor yet the other Apostles;
Not from the cannon's mouth were the tongues of fire they spake
    with!"
But unheeded fell this mild rebuke on the Captain,
Who had advanced to the table, and thus continued discoursing:
"Leave this matter to me, for to me by right it pertaineth.
War is a terrible trade; but in the cause that is righteous,
Sweet is the smell of powder; and thus I answer the challenge!"

   Then from the rattlesnake's skin, with a sudden, contemptuous
    gesture,
Jerking the Indian arrows, he filled it with powder and bullets
Full to the very jaws, and handed it back to the savage,
Saying, in thundering tones: "Here, take it! this is your answer!"
Silently out of the room then glided the glistening savage,
Bearing the serpent's skin, and seeming himself like a serpent,
Winding his sinuous way in the dark to the depths of the forest.

---

7 The poet here has used the words of John Robinson to the colonists after the
   first encounter with the Indians: "Oh, how happy a thing had it been, if you
   had converted some be fore you had killed any!"

V.

THE SAILING OF THE MAY FLOWER

Just in the gray of the dawn, as the mists up rose from the meadows,
There was a stir and a sound in the slumbering village of Plymouth;
Clanging and clicking of arms, and the order imperative, "Forward!"
Given in tone suppressed, a tramp of feet, and then silence.
Figures ten, in the mist, marched slowly out of the village.
Standish the stalwart it was, with eight of his valorous army,
Led by their Indian guide, by Hobomok, friend of the white men,
Northward marching to quell the sudden revolt of the savage.
Giants they seemed in the mist, or the mighty men of King David;
Giants in heart they were, who believed in God and the Bible, —
Ay, who believed in the smiting of Midianites and Philistines.
Over them gleamed far off the crimson banners of morning;
Under them loud on the sands, the serried billows, advancing,
Fired along the line, and in regular order retreated.

Many a mile had they marched, when at length the village of
    Plymouth
Woke from its sleep, and arose, intent on its manifold labors.
Sweet was the air and soft; and slowly the smoke from the chimneys
Rose over roofs of thatch, and pointed steadily eastward;
Men came forth from the doors, and paused and talked of the
    weather,
Said that the wind had changed, and was blowing fair for the May
    Flower;
Talked of their Captain's departure, and all the dangers that
    menaced,
He being gone, the town, and what should be done in his absence.
Merrily sang the birds, and the tender voices of women

Consecrated with hymns the common cares of the household.
Out of the sea rose the sun, and the billows rejoiced at his coming;
Beautiful were his feet on the purple tops of the mountains;
Beautiful on the sails of the May Flower riding at anchor,
Battered and blackened and worn by all the storms of the winter.
Loosely against her masts was hanging and flapping her canvas,
Rent by so many gales, and patched by the hands of the sailors.
Suddenly from her side, as the sun rose over the ocean,
Darted a puff of smoke, and floated seaward; anon rang
Loud over field and forest the cannon's roar, and the echoes
Heard and repeated the sound, the signal-gun of departure!
Ah! but with louder echoes replied the hearts of the people!
Meekly, in voices subdued, the chapter was read from the Bible,
Meekly the prayer was begun, but ended in fervent entreaty!
Then from their houses in haste came forth the Pilgrims of
        Plymouth,
Men and women and children, all hurrying down to the sea-shore,
Eager, with tearful eyes, to say farewell to the May Flower,
Homeward bound o'er the sea, and leaving them here in the desert.

Foremost among them was Alden. All night he had lain without
        slumber,
Turning and tossing about in the heat and unrest of his fever.
He had beheld Miles Standish, who came back late from the council,
Stalking into the room, and heard him mutter and murmur,
Sometimes it seemed a prayer, and sometimes it sounded like
        swearing.
Once he had come to the bed, and stood there a moment in silence;
Then he had turned away, and said: "I will not awake him;
Let him sleep on, it is best; for what is the use of more talking!"
Then he extinguished the light, and threw himself down on his
        pallet,
Dressed as he was, and ready to start at the break of the morning,—
Covered himself with the cloak he had worn in his campaigns in
        Flanders,—
Slept as a soldier sleeps in his bivouac, ready for action.

But with the dawn he arose; in the twilight Alden beheld him
Put on his corslet of steel, and all the rest of his armor,
Buckle about his waist his trusty blade of Damascus,
Take from the corner his musket, and so stride out of the chamber.
Often the heart of the youth had burned and yearned to embrace
   him,
Often his lips had essayed to speak, imploring for pardon;
All the old friendship came back, with its tender and grateful
   emotions;
But his pride overmastered the nobler nature within him,—
Pride, and the sense of his wrong, and the burning fire of the insult.
So he beheld his friend departing in anger, but spake not,
Saw him go forth to danger, perhaps to death, and he spake not!
Then he arose from his bed, and heard what the people were saying,
Joined in the talk at the door, with Stephen and Richard and
   Gilbert,[1]
Joined in the morning prayer, and in the reading of Scripture,
And, with the others, in haste went hurrying down to the sea-shore,
Down to the Plymouth Rock, that had been to their feet as a
   door-step
Into a world unknown, —the corner-stone of a nation!

   There with his boat was the Master, already a little impatient
Lest he should lose the tide, or the wind might shift to the eastward,
Square-built, hearty, and strong, with an odor of ocean about him,
Speaking with this one and that, and cramming letters and parcels
Into his pockets capacious, and messages mingled together
Into his narrow brain, till at last he was wholly bewildered.
Nearer the boat stood Alden, with one foot placed on the gunwale,
One still firm on the rock, and talking at times with the sailors,
Seated erect on the thwarts, all ready and eager for starting
He too was eager to go, and thus put an end to his anguish,

---

1   The names are not taken at random. Stephen Hopkins, Richard Warren, and
    Gilbert Winslow were all among the Mayflower passengers, and were alive at
    this time.

Thinking to fly from despair, that swifter than keel is or canvas,
Thinking to drown in the sea the ghost that would rise and pur-
    sue him.
But as he gazed on the crowd, he beheld the form of Priscilla
Standing dejected among them, unconscious of all that was passing
Fixed were her eyes upon his, as if she divined his intention,
Fixed with a look so sad, so reproachful, imploring, and patient,
That with a sudden revulsion his heart recoiled from its purpose,
As from the verge of a crag, where one step more is destruction.
Strange is the heart of man, with its quick, mysterious instincts!
Strange is the life of man, and fatal or fated are moments,
Whereupon turn, as on hinges, the gates of the wall adamantine!
"Here I remain!" he exclaimed, as he looked at the heavens above
    him,
Thanking the Lord whose breath had scattered the mist and the
    madness,
Wherein, blind and lost, to death he was staggering headlong.
"Yonder snow-white cloud, that floats in the ether above me,
Seems like a hand that is pointing and beckoning over the ocean.
There is another hand, that is not so spectral and ghost-like,
Holding me, drawing me back, and clasping mine for protection.
Float, O hand of cloud, and vanish away in the ether!
Roll thyself up like a fist, to threaten and daunt me; I heed not
Either your warning or menace, or any omen of evil!
There is no land so sacred, no air so pure and so wholesome,
As is the air she breathes, and the soil that is pressed by her
    footsteps.
Here for her sake will I stay, and like an invisible presence
Hover around her for ever, protecting, supporting her weakness;
Yes! as my foot was the first that stepped on this rock at the landing,
So, with the blessing of God, shall it be the last at the leaving!"

    Meanwhile the Master alert, but with dignified air and important,
Scanning with watchful eye the tide and the wind and the weather,
Walked about on the sands; and the people crowded around him
Saying a few last words, and enforcing his careful remembrance

Then, taking each by the hand, as if he were grasping a tiller,
Into the boat he sprang, and in haste shoved off to his vessel,
Glad in his heart to get rid of all this worry and flurry,
Glad to be gone from a land of sand and sickness and sorrow,
Short allowance of victual, and plenty of nothing but Gospel!
Lost in the sound of the oars was the last farewell of the Pilgrims!
O strong hearts and true! not one went back in the May Flower!
No, not one looked back, who had set his hand to this ploughing!

Soon were heard on board the shouts and songs of the sailors
Heaving the windlass round, and hoisting the ponderous anchor.
Then the yards were braced, and all sails set to the west-wind,
Blowing steady and strong; and the May Flower sailed from the
       harbor,
Rounded the point of the Gurnet,[2] and leaving far to the southward
Island and cape of sand, and the Field of the First Encounter,[3]
Took the wind on her quarter, and stood for the open Atlantic,
Borne on the send of the sea, and the swelling hearts of the Pilgrims.

Long in silence they watched the receding sail of the vessel,
Much endeared to them all, as something living and human;
Then, as if filled with the spirit, and wrapt in a vision prophetic,
Baring his hoary head, the excellent Elder of Plymouth
Said, "Let us pray!" and they prayed, and thanked the Lord and
       took courage.
Mournfully sobbed the waves at the base of the rock, and above
       them

---

2 The Gurnet, or Gurnet's Nose, is a headland connecting with Marshfield by a
   beach about seven miles long. On its southern extremity are two light-houses
   which light the entrance to Plymouth Harbor.
3 So after we had given God thanks for our deliverance, we took our shallop and
   went on our journey, and called this place The First Encounter." Bradford and
   Winslow's *Journal* in Young's *Chronicles*, p. 159. The place on the Eastham shore
   marked the spot where the Pilgrims had their first encounter with the Indians,
   December 8, 1620. A party under Miles Standish was exploring the country
   while the Mayflower was at anchor in Provincetown Harbor.

Bowed and whispered the wheat on the hill of death, and their
    kindred
Seemed to awake in their graves, and to join in the prayer that
    they uttered.
Sun-illumined and white, on the eastern verge of the ocean
Gleamed the departing sail, like a marble slab in a graveyard;
Buried beneath it lay for ever all hope of escaping.
Lo! as they turned to depart, they saw the form of an Indian,
Watching them from the hill; but while they spake with each other,
Pointing with outstretched hands, and saying, "Look!" he had
    vanished.
So they returned to their homes; but Alden lingered a little,
Musing alone on the shore, and watching the wash of the billows
Round the base of the rock, and the sparkle and flash of the
    sunshine,
Like the spirit of God, moving visibly over the waters.[4]

---

4   See Genesis i. 2.

VI.

PRISCILLA

Thus for a while he stood, and mused by the shore of the ocean,
Thinking of many things, and most of all of Priscilla;
And as if thought had the power to draw to itself, like the loadstone,
Whatsoever it touches, by subtile laws of its nature,
Lo! as he turned to depart, Priscilla was standing beside him.

"Are you so much offended, you will not speak to me?" said she.
"Am I so much to blame, that yesterday, when you were pleading
Warmly the cause of another, my heart, impulsive and wayward,
Pleaded your own, and spake out, forgetful perhaps of decorum?
Certainly you can forgive me for speaking so frankly, for saying
What I ought not to have said, yet now I can never unsay it;
For there are moments in life, when the heart is so full of emotion,
That if by chance it be shaken, or into its depths like a pebble
Drops some careless word, it overflows, and its secret,
Spilt on the ground like water, can never be gathered together.
Yesterday I was shocked, when I heard you speak of Miles Standish,
Praising his virtues, transforming his very defects into virtues,
Praising his courage and strength, and even his fighting in Flanders,
As if by fighting alone you could win the heart of a woman,
Quite overlooking yourself and the rest, in exalting your hero.
Therefore I spake as I did, by an irresistible impulse.
You will forgive me, I hope, for the sake of the friendship between
    us,
Which is too true and too sacred to be so easily broken!"
Thereupon answered John Alden, the scholar, the friend of Miles
    Standish:
"I was not angry with you, with myself alone I was angry,

45

Seeing how badly I managed the matter I had in my keeping."
"No!" interrupted the maiden, with answer prompt and decisive;
"No; you were angry with me, for speaking so frankly and freely.
It was wrong, I acknowledge; for it is the fate of a woman
Long to be patient and silent, to wait like a ghost that is speechless,
Till some questioning voice dissolves the spell of its silence.
Hence is the inner life of so many suffering women
Sunless and silent and deep, like subterranean rivers[1]
Running through caverns of darkness, unheard, unseen, and
    unfruitful,
Chafing their channels of stone, with endless and profitless
    murmurs."
Thereupon answered John Alden, the young man, the lover of
    women:
"Heaven forbid it, Priscilla; and truly they seem to me always
More like the beautiful rivers that watered the garden of Eden,
More like the river Euphrates, through deserts of Havilah flowing,
Filling the land with delight, and memories sweet of the garden!"
"Ah, by these words, I can see," again interrupted the maiden,
"How very little you prize me, or care for what I am saying.
When from the depths of my heart, in pain and with secret
    misgiving,
Frankly I speak to you, asking for sympathy only and kindness,
Straightway you take up my words, that are plain and direct and
    in earnest,
Turn them away from their meaning, and answer with flattering
    phrases.
This is not right, is not just, is not true to the best that is in you;
For I know and esteem you, and feel that your nature is noble,
Lifting mine up to a higher, a more ethereal level.

---

1 Compare Coleridge,—
    "Where Alph, the sacred river, ran
    Through caverns measureless to man,
    Down to a sunless sea."

                        Vision of Kubla Khan.

Therefore I value your friendship, and feel it perhaps the more
    keenly
If you say aught that implies I am only as one among many,
If you make use of those common and complimentary phrases
Most men think so fine, in dealing and speaking with women,
But which women reject as insipid, if not as insulting."

  Mute and amazed was Alden; and listened and looked at Priscilla,
Thinking he never had seen her more fair, more divine in her
    beauty.
He who but yesterday pleaded so glibly the cause of another,
Stood there embarrassed and silent, and seeking in vain for an
    answer.
So the maiden went on, and little divined or imagined
What was at work in his heart, that made him so awkward and
    speechless.
"Let us, then, be what we are, and speak what we think, and in
    all things
Keep ourselves loyal to truth, and the sacred professions of
    friendship.
It is no secret I tell you, nor am I ashamed to declare it:
I have liked to be with you, to see you, to speak with you always.
So I was hurt at your words, and a little affronted to hear you
Urge me to marry your friend, though he were the Captain Miles
    Standish.
For I must tell you the truth: much more to me is your friendship
Than all the love he could give, were he twice the hero you think
    him."
Then she extended her hand, and Alden, who eagerly grasped it,
Felt all the wounds in his heart, that were aching and bleeding
    so sorely,
Healed by the touch of that hand, and he said, with a voice full
    of feeling:
"Yes, we must ever be friends; and of all who offer you friendship
Let me be ever the first, the truest, the nearest and dearest!"

Casting a farewell look at the glimmering sail of the May Flower,
Distant, but still in sight, and sinking below the horizon,
Homeward together they walked, with a strange, indefinite feeling,
That all the rest had departed and left them alone in the desert.
But, as they went through the fields in the blessing and smile of
    the sunshine,
Lighter grew their hearts, and Priscilla said very archly:
"Now that our terrible Captain has gone in pursuit of the Indians,
Where he is happier far than he would be commanding a household,
You may speak boldly, and tell me of all that happened between you,
When you returned last night, and said how ungrateful you found
    me."
Thereupon answered John Alden, and told her the whole of the
    story,—
Told her his own despair, and the direful wrath of Miles Standish.
Whereat the maiden smiled, and said between laughing and earnest,
"He is a little chimney, and heated hot in a moment!"
But as he gently rebuked her, and told her how much he had
    suffered,
How he had even determined to sail that day in the May Flower,
And had remained for her sake, on hearing the dangers that
    threatened,
All her manner was changed, and she said with a faltering accent,
"Truly I thank you for this: how good you have been to me always!"

Thus, as a pilgrim devout, who toward Jerusalem journeys,
Taking three steps in advance, and one reluctantly backward,
Urged by importunate zeal, and withheld by pangs of contrition;
Slowly but steadily onward, receding yet ever advancing,
Journeyed this Puritan youth to the Holy Land of his longings,
Urged by the fervor of love, and withheld by remorseful misgivings.

VII.

THE MARCH OF MILES STANDISH

MEANWHILE the stalwart Miles Standish was marching steadily
    northward,
Winding through forest and swamp, and along the trend of the
    sea-shore,
All day long, with hardly a halt, the fire of his anger
Burning and crackling within, and the sulphurous odor of powder
Seeming more sweet to his nostrils than all the scents of the forest.
Silent and moody he went, and much he revolved his discomfort;
He who was used to success, and to easy victories always,
Thus to be flouted, rejected, and laughed to scorn by a maiden,
Thus to be mocked and betrayed by the friend whom most he had
    trusted!
Ah! 'twas too much to be borne, and he fretted and chafed in his
    armor!

"I alone am to blame," he muttered," for mine was the folly.
What has a rough old soldier, grown grim and gray in the harness,
Used to the camp and its ways, to do with the wooing of maidens?
'Twas but a dream, —let it pass—let it vanish like so many others!
What I thought was a flower, is only a weed, and is worthless;
Out of my heart will I pluck it, and throw it away, and hencefor-
    ward let it pass,
Be but a fighter of battles, a lover and wooer of dangers!"
Thus he revolved in his mind his sorry defeat and discomfort,
While he was marching by day or lying at night in the forest
Looking up at the trees, and the constellations beyond them.

After a three days' march he came to an Indian encampment[1]

---

1   The poet has taken his material for this expedition of Standish's from the report
    in Winslow's Relation of *Standish's Expedition against the Indians of Weymouth,*

49

Pitched on the edge of a meadow, between the sea and the forest;
Women at work by the tents, and the warriors, horrid with
    war-paint,
Seated about a fire, and smoking and talking together;
Who, when they saw from afar the sudden approach of the white
    men,
Saw the flash of the sun on breastplate and sabre and musket,
Straightway leaped to their feet, and two, from among them
    advancing,
Came to parley with Standish, and offer him furs as a present;
Friendship was in their looks, but in their hearts there was hatred.
Braves of the tribe were these, and brothers gigantic in stature,
Huge as Goliath of Gath, or the terrible Og, king of Bashan;
One was Pecksuot named, and the other was called Wattawamat.
Round their necks were suspended their knives in scabbards of
    wampum,
Two-edged, trenchant knives, with points as sharp as a needle.
Other arms had they none, for they were cunning and crafty
"Welcome, English!" they said, —these words they had learned
    from the traders
Touching at times on the coast, to barter and chaffer for peltries.
Then in their native tongue they began to parley with Standish,
Through his guide and interpreter, Hobomok, friend of the white
    man,
Begging for blankets and knives, but mostly for muskets and
    powder,
Kept by the white man, they said, concealed, with the plague, in
    his cellars,
Ready to be let loose, and destroy his brother the red man!
But when Standish refused, and said he would give them the Bible,
Suddenly changing their tone, they began to boast and to bluster.
Then Wattawamat advanced with a stride in front of the other,
And, with a lofty demeanor, thus vauntingly spake to the Captain:
"Now Wattawamat can see, by the fiery eyes of the Captain,

and the breaking up of Weston's Colony at that place, in March, 1623, as given in Dr. Young's *Chronicles.*

Angry is he in his heart; but the heart of the brave Wattawamat
Is not afraid at the sight. He was not born of a woman,
But on a mountain, at night, from an oak-tree riven by lightning,
Forth he sprang at a bound, with all his weapons about him,[2]
Shouting, 'Who is there here to fight with the brave Wattawamat?'"
Then he unsheathed his knife, and, whetting the blade on his left
    hand,
Held it aloft and displayed a woman's face on the handle,
Saying, with bitter expression and look of sinister meaning:
"I have another at home, with the face of a man on the handle;
By and by they shall marry; and there will be plenty of children!"

Then stood Pecksuot forth, self-vaunting, insulting Miles
    Standish:
While with his fingers he patted the knife that hung at his bosom,
Drawing it half from its sheath, and plunging it back, as he
    muttered,
"By and by it shall see; it shall eat; ah, ha! but shall speak not!
This is the mighty Captain the white men have sent to destroy us!
He is a little man ; let him go and work with the women!"

Meanwhile Standish had noted the faces and figures of Indians
Peeping and creeping about from bush to tree in the forest,
Feigning to look for game, with arrows set on their bow-strings,
Drawing about him still closer and closer the net of their ambush
But undaunted he stood, and dissembled and treated them smoothly;

---

2   "Among the rest Wituwamat bragged of the excellency of his knife. On the end
of the handle there was pictured a woman's face ; but,' said he, I have another at home wherewith I have killed both French and English, and that hath a
man's face on it, and by and by these two must marry.' Further he said of that
knife he there had, *Hinnaim namen, hinnaim michen, matta cuts*; that is to say, By
and by it should see, and by and by it should eat, but not speak. Also Pecksuot,
being a man of greater stature than the captain, told him, though he were a
great captain, yet he was but a little man ; and, said he, though I be no sachem,
yet I am a man of great strength and courage." Winslow's *Relation*. The poet
turns the whole incident of Standish's parley and killing of the Indians into a
more open and brave piece of conduct than the chronicle admits.

So the old chronicles say, that were writ in the days of the fathers
But when he heard their defiance, the boast, the taunt, and the
    insult,
All the hot blood of his race, of Sir Hugh and of Thurston de
    Standish,
Boiled and beat in his heart, and swelled in the veins of his temples.
Headlong he leaped on the boaster, and, snatching his knife from
    its scabbard,
Plunged it into his heart, and, reeling backward, the savage
Fell with his face to the sky, and a fiendlike fierceness upon it.
Straight there arose from the forest the awful sound of the
    war-whoop,
And, like a flurry of snow on the whistling wind of December,
Swift and sudden and keen came a flight of feathery arrows.
Then came a cloud of smoke, and out of the cloud came the
    lightning,
Out of the lightning thunder; and death unseen ran before it.
Frightened the savages fled for shelter in swamp and in thicket,
Hotly pursued and beset; but their sachem,the brave Wattawamat,
Fled not; he was dead. Unswerving and swift had a bullet
Passed through his brain, and he fell with both hands clutching
    the greensward,
Seeming in death to hold back from his foe the land of his fathers.

    There on the flowers of the meadow the warriors lay, and above
    them,
Silent, with folded arms, stood Hobomok, friend of the white man.[3]
Smiling at length he exclaimed to the stalwart Captain of Plymouth:
"Pecksuot bragged very loud, of his courage, his strength, and
    his stature,—

---

3 "Hobbamock stood by all this time as a spectator, and meddled not, observ-
   ing how our men demeaned themselves in this action. All being here ended,
   smiling, he brake forth into these speeches to the Captain : Yesterday Pecksuot,
   bragging of his own strength and stature, said, though you were a great captain, yet you were but a little man ; but to-day I see you are big enough to lay
   him on the ground.'" Winslow's *Relation.*

"Held it aloft and displayed a woman's face on the handle"

Mocked the great Captain, and called him a little man; but I see now
Big enough have you been to lay him speechless before you!"

   Thus the first battle was fought and won by the stalwart Miles
       Standish.
When the tidings thereof were brought to the village of Plymouth,
And as a trophy of war the head of the brave Wattawamat[4]
Scowled from the roof of the fort, which at once was a church
       and a fortress,
All who beheld it rejoiced, and praised the Lord, and took courage.
Only Priscilla averted her face from this spectre of terror,
Thanking God in her heart that she had not married Miles Standish;
Shrinking, fearing almost, lest, coming home from his battles,
He should lay claim to her hand, as the prize and reward of his
       valor.

---

4   "Now was the Captain returned and received with joy, the head being brought
    to the fort, and there set up." Winslow's *Relation*. The custom of exposing the
    heads of offenders in this way was familiar enough to the Plymouth people be-
    fore they left England. As late as the year 1747 the heads of the lords who were
    concerned in the Scots' Rebellion were set up over Temple Bar, in London.

VIII.

THE SPINNING-WHEEL

MONTH after month passed away, and in Autumn the ships of
    the merchants
Came with kindred and friends, with cattle and corn for the
    Pilgrims.[1]
All in the village was peace; the men were intent on their labors,
Busy with hewing and building, with garden plot and with
    merestead,[2]
Busy with breaking the glebe, and mowing the grass in the meadows,
Searching the sea for its fish, and hunting the deer in the forest.
All in the village was peace; but at times the rumor of warfare
Filled the air with alarm, and the apprehension of danger.
Bravely the stalwart Miles Standish was scouring the land with
    his forces,
Waxing valiant in fight and defeating the alien armies,
Till his name had become a sound of fear to the nations.
Anger was still in his heart, but at times the remorse and contrition
Which in all noble natures succeed the passionate outbreak,
Came like a rising tide, that encounters the rush of a river,
Staying its current awhile, but making it bitter and brackish.

    Meanwhile Alden at home had built him a new habitation,
Solid, substantial, of timber rough-hewn from the firs of the forest.
Wooden-barred was the door, and the roof was covered with rushes;

---

1   The poet again has moved the narrative forward, taking Standish's return from
    his expedition as the date from which after events are measured. The Anne and
    the Little James came at the beginning of August, 1623.
2   *Mere* or *meare* in Old English is boundary, and *merestead* becomes the bound-
    ed lot. The first entry in the records of Plymouth Colony is an incomplete list
    of "The Meersteads and Garden-plotes of those which came first, layed out,
    1620."

Latticed the windows were, and the window panes were of paper,[3]
Oiled to admit the light, while wind and rain were excluded.
There too he dug a well, and around it planted an orchard:
Still may be seen to this day some trace of the well and the orchard.[4]
Close to the house was the stall, where, safe and secure from
    annoyance,
Raghorn, the snow-white steer, that had fallen to Alden's allotment
In the division of cattle, might ruminate in the night-time
Over the pastures he cropped, made fragrant by sweet pennyroyal.

   Oft when his labor was finished, with eager feet would the
    dreamer
Follow the pathway that ran through the woods to the house of
    Priscilla,
Led by illusions romantic and subtile deceptions of fancy,
Pleasure disguised as duty, and love in the semblance of friendship.
Ever of her he thought, when he fashioned the walls of his dwelling;
Ever of her he thought, when he delved in the soil of his garden;
Ever of her he thought, when he read in his Bible on Sunday
Praise of the virtuous woman, as she is described in the Proverbs,—
How the heart of her husband doth safely trust in her always,
How all the days of her life she will do him good, and not evil,
How she seeketh the wool and the flax and worketh with gladness,
How she layeth her hand to the spindle and holdeth the distaff,
How she is not afraid of the snow for herself or her household,
Knowing her household are clothed with the scarlet cloth of her
    weaving!

---

3 When the Fortune, which visited the colony in November, 1621, returned to
    England, Edward Winslow wrote by it a letter of advice to those who were
    thinking of emigrating to America, in which he says, "Bring paper and linseed
    oil for your windows." Glass windows were long considered a great luxury.
    When the Duke of Northumberland, in Elizabeth's time, left Alnwick Castle
    to come to London for the winter, the few glass windows which formed one
    of the luxuries of the castle were carefully taken out and laid away, perhaps
    carried to London to adorn the city residence.
4 The Alden family still retain John Alden's homestead in Duxbury, and the
    present house is said to stand on the site of the one originally built there.

So as she sat at her wheel one afternoon in the Autumn,
Alden, who opposite sat, and was watching her dexterous fingers,
As if the thread she was spinning were that of his life and his
    fortune,
After a pause in their talk, thus spake to the sound of the spindle.
"Truly, Priscilla," he said, "when I see you spinning and spinning,
Never idle a moment, but thrifty and thoughtful of others,
Suddenly you are transformed, are visibly changed in a moment;
You are no longer Priscilla, but Bertha the Beautiful Spinner."[5]
Here the light foot on the treadle grew swifter and swifter; the
    spindle
Uttered an angry snarl, and the thread snapped short in her fingers;
While the impetuous speaker, not heeding the mischief, continued:
"You are the beautiful Bertha, the spinner, the queen of Helvetia;
She whose story I read at a stall in the streets of Southampton,
Who, as she rode on her palfrey, o'er valley and meadow and
    mountain,
Ever was spinning her thread from a distaff fixed to her saddle.
She was so thrifty and good, that her name passed into a proverb.
So shall it be with your own, when the spinning-wheel shall no
    longer
Hum in the house of the farmer, and fill its chambers with music
Then shall the mothers, reproving, relate how it was in their
    childhood,
Praising the good old times, and the days of Priscilla the spinner!"
Straight up rose from her wheel the beautiful Puritan maiden,
Pleased with the praise of her thrift from him whose praise was
    the sweetest,
Drew from the reel on the table a snowy skein of her spinning,
Thus making answer, meanwhile, to the flattering phrases of Alden:
"Come, you must not be idle; if I am a pattern for housewives,
Show yourself equally worthy of being the model of husbands.
Hold this skein on your hands, while I wind it, ready for knitting;

---

5   The legend of Bertha is given with various learning regarding it in a mono-
graph entitled, *Bertha die Spinnerin*, by Karl Joseph Simrock, Frankfurt, 1853.

Then who knows but hereafter, when fashions have changed and
    the manners,
Fathers may talk to their sons of the good old times of John Alden!"
Thus, with a jest and a laugh, the skein on his hands she adjusted,
He sitting awkwardly there, with his arms extended before him,
She standing graceful, erect, and winding the thread from his
    fingers,
Sometimes chiding a little his clumsy manner of holding,
Sometimes touching his hands, as she disentangled expertly
Twist or knot in the yarn, unawares —for how could she help it?—
Sending electrical thrills through every nerve in his body.

   Lo! in the midst of this scene, a breathless messenger entered,
Bringing in hurry and heat the terrible news from the village.
Yes; Miles Standish was dead! —an Indian had brought them the
    tidings,—
Slain by a poisoned arrow, shot down in the front of the battle,
Into an ambush beguiled, cut off with the whole of his forces;
All the town would be burned, and all the people be murdered!
Such were the tidings of evil that burst on the hearts of the hearers.
Silent and statue-like stood Priscilla, her face looking backward
Still at the face of the speaker, her arms up lifted in horror;
But John Alden, upstarting, as if the barb of the arrow
Piercing the heart of his friend had struck his own, and had
    sundered
Once and for ever the bonds that held him bound as a captive,
Wild with excess of sensation, the awful delight of his freedom,
Mingled with pain and regret, unconscious of what he was doing,
Clasped, almost with a groan, the motionless form of Priscilla,
Pressing her close to his heart, as for ever his own, and exclaiming:
"Those whom the Lord hath united, let no man put them asunder!"

   Even as rivulets. twain, from distant and separate sources,
Seeing each other afar, as they leap from the rocks, and pursuing
Each one its devious path, but drawing nearer and nearer,
Rush together at last, at their trysting-place in the forest;

So these lives that had run thus far in separate channels,
Coming in sight of each other, then swerving and flowing asunder,
Parted by barriers strong, but drawing nearer and nearer,
Rushed together at last, and one was lost in the other.

THE BRIDAL PROCESSION

IX.

THE WEDDING-DAY

FORTH from the curtain of clouds, from the tent of purple and
    scarlet,
Issued the sun, the great High-Priest, in his garments resplendent,[1]
Holiness unto the Lord, in letters of light, on his forehead,
Round the hem of his robe the golden bells and pomegranates.
Blessing the world he came, and the bars of vapor beneath him
Gleamed like a grate of brass, and the sea at his feet was a laver!

This was the wedding morn of Priscilla the Puritan maiden.
Friends were assembled together; the Elder and Magistrate also
Graced the scene with their presence, and stood like the Law and
    the Gospel,
One with the sanction of earth and one with the blessing of heaven.
Simple and brief was the wedding, as that of Ruth and of Boaz.
Softly the youth and the maiden repeated the words of betrothal,
Taking each other for husband and wife in the Magistrate's
    presence,
After the Puritan way, and the laudable custom of Holland.[2]
Fervently then, and devoutly, the excellent Elder of Plymouth
Prayed for the hearth and the home, that were founded that day
    in affection,

---

1   For a description of the Jewish high-priest and his dress, see Exodus, chapter
    xxviii,
2   "May 12 was the first marriage in this place, which, according to the laudable
    custome of the Low-Countries, in which they had lived, was thought most
    requisite to be performed by the magistrate, as being a civil thing, upon which
    many questions aboute inheritances doe depende, with other things most
    proper to their cognizans, and most consonante to the scriptures, Ruth 4, and
    nowhere found in the gospell to be layed on the ministers as a part of their
    office." Bradford's *History*, p. 101

Speaking of life and of death, and imploring divine benedictions.

Lo! when the service was ended, a form appeared on the threshold,
Clad in armor of steel, a sombre and sorrowful figure!
Why does the bridegroom start and stare at the strange apparition?
Why does the bride turn pale, and hide her face on his shoulder?
Is it a phantom of air, —a bodiless, spectral illusion?
Is it a ghost from the grave, that has come to forbid the betrothal?
Long had it stood there unseen, a guest uninvited, unwelcomed;
Over its clouded eyes there had passed at times an expression
Softening the gloom and revealing the warm heart hidden beneath
    them,
As when across the sky the driving rack[3] of the rain-cloud
Grows for a moment thin, and betrays the sun by its brightness.
Once it had lifted its hand, and moved its lips, but was silent,
As if an iron will had mastered the fleeting intention.
But when were ended the troth and the prayer and the last
    benediction,
Into the room it strode, and the people beheld with amazement
Bodily there in his armor Miles Standish, the Captain of Plymouth!
Grasping the bridegroom's hand, he said with emotion,
"Forgive me! I have been angry and hurt, —too long have
    I cherished the feeling;
I have been cruel and hard, but now, thank God! it is ended.
Mine is the same hot blood that leaped in the veins of Hugh
    Standish,
Sensitive, swift to resent, but as swift in atoning for error.

---

3   Rack, a Shaksperian word, used possibly in two senses, either as vapor, as in
    the thirty-third sonnet,—
        "Anon permit the basest clouds to ride
        With ugly rack on his celestial face,"
    which is plainly the meaning here, or as a light, cirrus cloud, as in the *Tempest*,
        Act IV. Scene 1;—
        "And like this insubstantial pageant faded,
        Leave not a rack behind,"
    although here, also, the meaning of vapor might be admissible. Bacon has de-
    fined rack: "The winds, which wave the clouds above, which we call the rack,
    and are not perceived below, pass without noise."

Never so much as now was Miles Standish the friend of John Alden."
Thereupon answered the bridegroom: "Let all be forgotten between
    us,—
All save the dear, old friendship, and that shall grow older and
    dearer!"
Then the Captain advanced, and, bowing, saluted Priscilla,
Gravely, and after the manner of old-fashioned gentry in England,
Something of camp and of court, of town and of country,
    commingled,
Wishing her joy of her wedding, and loudly lauding her husband.
Then he said with a smile: "I should have remembered the adage,—
If you would be well served, you must serve yourself; and moreover,
No man can gather cherries in Kent at the season of Christmas!"

    Great was the people's amazement, and greater yet their rejoicing,
Thus to behold once more the sun-burnt face of their Captain,
Whom they had mourned as dead; and they gathered and crowded
    about him,
Eager to see him and hear him, forgetful of bride and of bridegroom,
Questioning, answering, laughing, and each interrupting the other,
Till the good Captain declared, being quite overpowered and
    bewildered,
He had rather by far break into an Indian encampment,
Than come again to a wedding to which he had not been invited.

    Meanwhile the bridegroom went forth and stood with the bride
    at the doorway,
Breathing the perfumed air of that warm and beautiful morning.
Touched with autumnal tints, but lonely and sad in the sunshine,
Lay extended before them the land of toil and privation;
There were the graves of the dead, and the barren waste of the
    sea-shore,
There the familiar fields, the groves of pine, and the meadows;
But to their eyes transfigured, it seemed as the Garden of Eden,
Filled with the presence of God, whose voice was the sound of
    the ocean.

Soon was their vision disturbed by the noise and stir of departure,
Friends coming forth from the house, and impatient of longer
    delaying,
Each with his plan for the day, and the work that was left
    uncompleted.
Then from a stall near at hand, amid exclamations of wonder,
Alden the thoughtful, the careful, so happy, so proud of Priscilla,
Brought out his snow-white steer, obeying the hand of its master,
Led by a cord that was tied to an iron ring in its nostrils,
Covered with crimson cloth, and a cushion placed for a saddle.
She should not walk, he said, through the dust and heat of the
    noonday;
Nay, she should ride like a queen, not plod along like a peasant.
Somewhat alarmed at first, but reassured by the others,
Placing her hand on the cushion, her foot in the hand of her
    husband,
Gayly, with joyous laugh, Priscilla mounted her palfrey.
"Nothing is wanting now," he said with a smile, "but the distaff;
Then you would be in truth my queen, my beautiful Bertha!"

Onward the bridal procession now moved to their new habitation,
Happy husband and wife, and friends conversing together.
Pleasantly murmured the brook, as they crossed the ford in the
    forest,
Pleased with the image that passed, like a dream of love through
    its bosom,
Tremulous, floating in air, o'er the depths of the azure abysses.
Down through the golden leaves the sun was pouring his splendors,
Gleaming on purple grapes, that, from branches above them
    suspended,
Mingled their odorous breath with the balm of the pine and the
    fir-tree,
Wild and sweet as the clusters that grew in the valley of Eshcol.
Like a picture it seemed of the primitive, pastoral ages,

THE BRIDAL PROCESSION

Fresh with the youth of the world, and recalling Rebecca and Isaac,
Old and yet ever new, and simple and beautiful always,
Love immortal and young in the endless succession of lovers.
So through the Plymouth woods passed onward the bridal
    procession.

Note.

[Miles Standish was not inconsolable. In the Anne came a certain
Barbara, whose family name is unknown, but of whom there are vague traditions that she was a kinswoman of Rose Standish. The Captain and Barbara
were married, and had seven children, of whom four sons, Alexander, Miles,
Josiah, and Charles, survived their father. The only daughter, Lora, whose
sampler is one of the most interesting relics in the Memorial Hall at Plymouth,
died in her youth. Something of the old soldier's affectionate nature can be
seen in the will, drawn up when he was very ancient and full of dolorous
pains." Leaving his " dearly beloved wife, Barbara" and his elder sons, exec-
utors, he appoints two friends supervisors of his will, begging them to see
that his " poor wife shall have as comfortable maintenance as my poor state
will bear, the whole time of her life, which if you my loving friends please
to do, though neither they nor I shall be able to recompense, I do not doubt
but the Lord will." Also he leaves a legacy to the granddaughter of Robinson,
the Pilgrims' pastor at Leyden, "whom I tenderly love for her grandfather's
sake," and he directs that his body be laid "as near as may be to my two dear
daughters, Lora Standish, my daughter, and Mary Standish my daughter-
in-law." Mary (Dingley) was the wife of Josiah Standish ; his eldest brother,
Alexander, married Sarah, one of the daughters of John and Priscilla Alden.
The descendants of both Standish and Alden are very numerous.]

BIRDS OF PASSAGE

. . come i gru van cantando lor lai,
Facendo in aer di sè lunga riga.

DANTE.

PROMETHEUS,
OR THE POET'S FORETHOUGHT

Of Prometheus, how undaunted
    On Olympus' shining bastions
His audacious foot he planted,
Myths are told and songs are chanted,
    Full of promptings and suggestions.

Beautiful is the tradition
    Of that flight through heavenly portals,
The old classic superstition
Of the theft and the transmission
    Of the fire of the Immortals!

First the deed of noble daring,
    Born of heavenward aspiration,
Then the fire with mortals sharing,
Then the vulture,--the despairing
    Cry of pain on crags Caucasian.

All is but a symbol painted
    Of the Poet, Prophet, Seer;
Only those are crowned and sainted
Who with grief have been acquainted,
    Making nations nobler, freer.

In their feverish exultations,
    In their triumph and their yearning,
In their passionate pulsations,
In their words among the nations,
    The Promethean fire is burning.

Shall it, then, be unavailing,
   All this toil for human culture?
Through the cloud-rack, dark and trailing,
Must they see above them sailing
   O'er life's barren crags the vulture?

Such a fate as this was Dante's,
   By defeat and exile maddened;
Thus were Milton and Cervantes,
Nature's priests and Corybantes,
   By affliction touched and saddened.

But the glories so transcendent
   That around their memories cluster,
And, on all their steps attendant,
Make their darkened lives resplendent
   With such gleams of inward lustre!

All the melodies mysterious,
   Through the dreary darkness chanted;
Thoughts in attitudes imperious,
Voices soft, and deep, and serious,
   Words that whispered, songs that haunted!

All the soul in rapt suspension,
   All the quivering, palpitating
Chords of life in utmost tension,
With the fervor of invention,
   With the rapture of creating!

Ah, Prometheus! heaven-scaling!
   In such hours of exultation
Even the faintest heart, unquailing,
Might behold the vulture sailing
   Round the cloudy crags Caucasian!

Though to all there is not given
    Strength for such sublime endeavor,
Thus to scale the walls of heaven,
And to leaven with fiery leaven
    All the hearts of men forever;

Yet all bards, whose hearts unblighted
    Honor and believe the presage,
Hold aloft their torches lighted,
Gleaming through the realms benighted,
    As they onward bear the message!

THE LADDER OF ST. AUGUSTINE

Saint Augustine! well hast thou said,
    That of our vices we can frame
A ladder, if we will but tread
    Beneath our feet each deed of shame!

All common things, each day's events,
    That with the hour begin and end,
Our pleasures and our discontents,
    Are rounds by which we may ascend.

The low desire, the base design,
    That makes another's virtues less;
The revel of the ruddy wine,
    And all occasions of excess;

The longing for ignoble things;
    The strife for triumph more than truth;
The hardening of the heart, that brings
    Irreverence for the dreams of youth;

All thoughts of ill; all evil deeds,
    That have their root in thoughts of ill;
Whatever hinders or impedes
    The action of the nobler will;—

All these must first be trampled down
    Beneath our feet, if we would gain
In the bright fields of fair renown
    The right of eminent domain.

We have not wings, we cannot soar;
   But we have feet to scale and climb
By slow degrees, by more and more,
   The cloudy summits of our time.

The mighty pyramids of stone
   That wedge-like cleave the desert airs,
When nearer seen, and better known,
   Are but gigantic flights of stairs.

The distant mountains, that uprear
   Their solid bastions to the skies,
Are crossed by pathways, that appear
   As we to higher levels rise.

The heights by great men reached and kept
   Were not attained by sudden flight,
But they, while their companions slept,
   Were toiling upward in the night.

Standing on what too long we bore
   With shoulders bent and downcast eyes,
We may discern--unseen before--
   A path to higher destinies.

Nor deem the irrevocable Past,
   As wholly wasted, wholly vain,
If, rising on its wrecks, at last
   To something nobler we attain.

THE PHANTOM SHIP

In Mather's Magnalia Christi,
    Of the old colonial time,
May be found in prose the legend
    That is here set down in rhyme.

A ship sailed from New Haven,
    And the keen and frosty airs,
That filled her sails at parting,
    Were heavy with good men's prayers.

"O Lord! if it be thy pleasure"—
    Thus prayed the old divine—
"To bury our friends in the ocean,
    Take them, for they are thine!"

But Master Lamberton muttered,
    And under his breath said he,
"This ship is so crank and walty
    I fear our grave she will be!"

And the ships that came from England,
    When the winter months were gone,
Brought no tidings of this vessel
    Nor of Master Lamberton.

This put the people to praying
    That the Lord would let them hear
What in his greater wisdom
    He had done with friends so dear.

And at last their prayers were answered:—
  It was in the month of June,
An hour before the sunset
  Of a windy afternoon,

When, steadily steering landward,
  A ship was seen below,
And they knew it was Lamberton, Master,
  Who sailed so long ago.

On she came, with a cloud of canvas,
  Right against the wind that blew,
Until the eye could distinguish
  The faces of the crew.

Then fell her straining topmasts,
  Hanging tangled in the shrouds,
And her sails were loosened and lifted,
  And blown away like clouds.

And the masts, with all their rigging,
  Fell slowly, one by one,
And the hulk dilated and vanished,
  As a sea-mist in the sun!

And the people who saw this marvel
  Each said unto his friend,
That this was the mould of their vessel,
  And thus her tragic end.

And the pastor of the village
  Gave thanks to God in prayer,
That, to quiet their troubled spirits,
  He had sent this Ship of Air.

THE WARDEN OF THE CINQUE PORTS

A mist was driving down the British Channel,
  The day was just begun,
And through the window-panes, on floor and panel,
  Streamed the red autumn sun.

It glanced on flowing flag and rippling pennon,
  And the white sails of ships;
And, from the frowning rampart, the black cannon
  Hailed it with feverish lips.

Sandwich and Romney, Hastings, Hithe, and Dover
  Were all alert that day,
To see the French war-steamers speeding over,
  When the fog cleared away.

Sullen and silent, and like couchant lions,
  Their cannon, through the night,
Holding their breath, had watched, in grim defiance,
  The sea-coast opposite.

And now they roared at drum-beat from their stations
  On every citadel;
Each answering each, with morning salutations,
  That all was well.

And down the coast, all taking up the burden,
  Replied the distant forts,
As if to summon from his sleep the Warden
  And Lord of the Cinque Ports.

Him shall no sunshine from the fields of azure,
  No drum-beat from the wall,
No morning gun from the black fort's embrasure,
  Awaken with its call!

No more, surveying with an eye impartial
  The long line of the coast,
Shall the gaunt figure of the old Field Marshal
  Be seen upon his post!

For in the night, unseen, a single warrior,
  In sombre harness mailed,
Dreaded of man, and surnamed the Destroyer,
  The rampart wall has scaled.

He passed into the chamber of the sleeper,
  The dark and silent room,
And as he entered, darker grew, and deeper,
  The silence and the gloom.

He did not pause to parley or dissemble,
  But smote the Warden hoar;
Ah! what a blow! that made all England tremble
  And groan from shore to shore.

Meanwhile, without, the surly cannon waited,
  The sun rose bright o'erhead;
Nothing in Nature's aspect intimated
  That a great man was dead.

HAUNTED HOUSES

All houses wherein men have lived and died
    Are haunted houses. Through the open doors
The harmless phantoms on their errands glide,
    With feet that make no sound upon the floors.

We meet them at the doorway, on the stair,
    Along the passages they come and go,
Impalpable impressions on the air,
    A sense of something moving to and fro.

There are more guests at table, than the hosts
    Invited; the illuminated hall
Is thronged with quiet, inoffensive ghosts,
    As silent as the pictures on the wall.

The stranger at my fireside cannot see
    The forms I see, nor hear the sounds I hear;
He but perceives what is; while unto me
    All that has been is visible and clear.

We have no title-deeds to house or lands;
    Owners and occupants of earlier dates
From graves forgotten stretch their dusty hands,
    And hold in mortmain still their old estates.

The spirit-world around this world of sense
    Floats like an atmosphere, and everywhere
Wafts through these earthly mists and vapors dense
    A vital breath of more ethereal air.

Our little lives are kept in equipoise
  By opposite attractions and desires;
The struggle of the instinct that enjoys,
  And the more noble instinct that aspires.

These perturbations, this perpetual jar
  Of earthly wants and aspirations high,
Come from the influence of an unseen star,
  An undiscovered planet in our sky.

And as the moon from some dark gate of cloud
  Throws o'er the sea a floating bridge of light,
Across whose trembling planks our fancies crowd
  Into the realm of mystery and night,—

So from the world of spirits there descends
  A bridge of light, connecting it with this,
O'er whose unsteady floor, that sways and bends,
  Wander our thoughts above the dark abyss.

IN THE CHURCHYARD AT CAMBRIDGE

In the village churchyard she lies,
Dust is in her beautiful eyes,
   No more she breathes, nor feels, nor stirs;
At her feet and at her head
Lies a slave to attend the dead,
   But their dust is white as hers.

Was she a lady of high degree,
So much in love with the vanity
   And foolish pomp of this world of ours?
Or was it Christian charity,
And lowliness and humility,
   The richest and rarest of all dowers?

Who shall tell us? No one speaks;
No color shoots into those cheeks,
   Either of anger or of pride,
At the rude question we have asked;
Nor will the mystery be unmasked
   By those who are sleeping at her side.

Hereafter? —And do you think to look
On the terrible pages of that Book
   To find her failings, faults, and errors?
Ah, you will then have other cares,
In your own short-comings and despairs,
   In your own secret sins and terrors!

THE EMPEROR'S BIRD'S-NEST

Once the Emperor Charles of Spain,
  With his swarthy, grave commanders,
I forget in what campaign,
Long besieged, in mud and rain,
  Some old frontier town of Flanders.

Up and down the dreary camp,
  In great boots of Spanish leather,
Striding with a measured tramp,
These Hidalgos, dull and damp,
  Cursed the Frenchmen, cursed the weather.

Thus as to and fro they went,
  Over upland and through hollow,
Giving their impatience vent,
Perched upon the Emperor's tent,
  In her nest, they spied a swallow.

Yes, it was a swallow's nest,
  Built of clay and hair of horses,
Mane, or tail, or dragoon's crest,
Found on hedge-rows east and west,
  After skirmish of the forces.

Then an old Hidalgo said,
  As he twirled his gray mustachio,
"Sure this swallow overhead
Thinks the Emperor's tent a shed,
  And the Emperor but a Macho!"

Hearing his imperial name
   Coupled with those words of malice,
Half in anger, half in shame,
Forth the great campaigner came
   Slowly from his canvas palace.

"Let no hand the bird molest,"
   Said he solemnly, "nor hurt her!"
Adding then, by way of jest,
"Golondrina is my guest,
   'T is the wife of some deserter!"

Swift as bowstring speeds a shaft,
   Through the camp was spread the rumor,
And the soldiers, as they quaffed
Flemish beer at dinner, laughed
   At the Emperor's pleasant humor.

So unharmed and unafraid
   Sat the swallow still and brooded,
Till the constant cannonade
Through the walls a breach had made,
   And the siege was thus concluded.

Then the army, elsewhere bent,
   Struck its tents as if disbanding,
Only not the Emperor's tent,
For he ordered, ere he went,
   Very curtly, "Leave it standing!"

So it stood there all alone,
   Loosely flapping, torn and tattered,
Till the brood was fledged and flown,
Singing o'er those walls of stone
   Which the cannon-shot had shattered.

THE TWO ANGELS

Two angels, one of Life and one of Death,
    Passed o'er our village as the morning broke;
The dawn was on their faces, and beneath,
    The sombre houses hearsed with plumes of smoke.

Their attitude and aspect were the same,
    Alike their features and their robes of white;
But one was crowned with amaranth, as with flame,
    And one with asphodels, like flakes of light.

I saw them pause on their celestial way;
    Then said I, with deep fear and doubt oppressed,
"Beat not so loud, my heart, lest thou betray
    The place where thy beloved are at rest!"

And he who wore the crown of asphodels,
    Descending, at my door began to knock,
And my soul sank within me, as in wells
    The waters sink before an earthquake's shock.

I recognized the nameless agony,
    The terror and the tremor and the pain,
That oft before had filled or haunted me,
    And now returned with threefold strength again.

The door I opened to my heavenly guest,
    And listened, for I thought I heard God's voice;
And, knowing whatsoe'er he sent was best,
    Dared neither to lament nor to rejoice.

Then with a smile, that filled the house with light,
   "My errand is not Death, but Life," he said;
And ere I answered, passing out of sight,
   On his celestial embassy he sped.

'T was at thy door, O friend! and not at mine,
   The angel with the amaranthine wreath,
Pausing, descended, and with voice divine,
   Whispered a word that had a sound like Death.

Then fell upon the house a sudden gloom,
   A shadow on those features fair and thin;
And softly, from that hushed and darkened room,
   Two angels issued, where but one went in.

All is of God! If he but wave his hand,
   The mists collect, the rain falls thick and loud,
Till, with a smile of light on sea and land,
   Lo! he looks back from the departing cloud.

Angels of Life and Death alike are his;
   Without his leave they pass no threshold o'er;
Who, then, would wish or dare, believing this,
   Against his messengers to shut the door?

DAYLIGHT AND MOONLIGHT

In broad daylight, and at noon,
Yesterday I saw the moon
Sailing high, but faint and white,
As a school-boy's paper kite.

In broad daylight, yesterday,
I read a Poet's mystic lay;
And it seemed to me at most
As a phantom, or a ghost.

But at length the feverish day
Like a passion died away,
And the night, serene and still,
Fell on village, vale, and hill.

Then the moon, in all her pride,
Like a spirit glorified,
Filled and overflowed the night
With revelations of her light.

And the Poet's song again
Passed like music through my brain;
Night interpreted to me
All its grace and mystery.

THE JEWISH CEMETERY AT NEWPORT

How strange it seems! These Hebrews in their graves,
    Close by the street of this fair seaport town,
Silent beside the never-silent waves,
    At rest in all this moving up and down!

The trees are white with dust, that o'er their sleep
    Wave their broad curtains in the south-wind's breath,
While underneath such leafy tents they keep
    The long, mysterious Exodus of Death.

And these sepulchral stones, so old and brown,
    That pave with level flags their burial-place,
Seem like the tablets of the Law, thrown down
    And broken by Moses at the mountain's base.

The very names recorded here are strange,
    Of foreign accent, and of different climes;
Alvares and Rivera interchange
    With Abraham and Jacob of old times.

"Blessed be God! for he created Death!"
    The mourners said, "and Death is rest and peace";
Then added, in the certainty of faith,
    "And giveth Life that never more shall cease."

Closed are the portals of their Synagogue,
    No Psalms of David now the silence break,
No Rabbi reads the ancient Decalogue
    In the grand dialect the Prophets spake.

Gone are the living, but the dead remain,
    And not neglected; for a hand unseen,
Scattering its bounty, like a summer rain,
    Still keeps their graves and their remembrance green.

How came they here? What burst of Christian hate,
    What persecution, merciless and blind,
Drove o'er the sea —that desert desolate—
    These Ishmaels and Hagars of mankind?

They lived in narrow streets and lanes obscure,
    Ghetto and Judenstrass, in mirk and mire;
Taught in the school of patience to endure
    The life of anguish and the death of fire.

All their lives long, with the unleavened bread
    And bitter herbs of exile and its fears,
The wasting famine of the heart they fed,
    And slaked its thirst with marah of their tears.

Anathema maranatha! was the cry
    That rang from town to town, from street to street;
At every gate the accursed Mordecai
    Was mocked and jeered, and spurned by Christian feet.

Pride and humiliation hand in hand
    Walked with them through the world where'er they went;
Trampled and beaten were they as the sand,
    And yet unshaken as the continent.

For in the background figures vague and vast
    Of patriarchs and of prophets rose sublime,
And all the great traditions of the Past
    They saw reflected in the coming time.

And thus forever with reverted look
   The mystic volume of the world they read,
Spelling it backward, like a Hebrew book,
   Till life became a Legend of the Dead.

But ah! what once has been shall be no more!
   The groaning earth in travail and in pain
Brings forth its races, but does not restore,
   And the dead nations never rise again.

OLIVER BASSELIN

In the Valley of the Vire
   Still is seen an ancient mill,
With its gables quaint and queer,
   And beneath the window-sill,
     On the stone,
     These words alone:
"Oliver Basselin lived here."

Far above it, on the steep,
   Ruined stands the old Chateau;
Nothing but the donjon-keep
   Left for shelter or for show.
     Its vacant eyes
     Stare at the skies,
Stare at the valley green and deep.

Once a convent, old and brown,
   Looked, but ah! it looks no more,
From the neighboring hillside down
   On the rushing and the roar
     Of the stream
     Whose sunny gleam
Cheers the little Norman town.

In that darksome mill of stone,
　　To the water's dash and din,
Careless, humble, and unknown,
　　Sang the poet Basselin
　　　　Songs that fill
　　　　That ancient mill
With a splendor of its own.

Never feeling of unrest
　　Broke the pleasant dream he dreamed;
Only made to be his nest,
　　All the lovely valley seemed;
　　　　No desire
　　　　Of soaring higher
Stirred or fluttered in his breast.

True, his songs were not divine;
　　Were not songs of that high art,
Which, as winds do in the pine,
　　Find an answer in each heart;
　　　　But the mirth
　　　　Of this green earth
Laughed and revelled in his line.

From the alehouse and the inn,
　　Opening on the narrow street,
Came the loud, convivial din,
　　Singing and applause of feet,
　　　　The laughing lays
　　　　That in those days
Sang the poet Basselin.

In the castle, cased in steel,
    Knights, who fought at Agincourt,
Watched and waited, spur on heel;
    But the poet sang for sport
        Songs that rang
        Another clang,
Songs that lowlier hearts could feel.

In the convent, clad in gray,
    Sat the monks in lonely cells,
Paced the cloisters, knelt to pray,
    And the poet heard their bells;
        But his rhymes
        Found other chimes,
Nearer to the earth than they.

Gone are all the barons bold,
    Gone are all the knights and squires,
Gone the abbot stern and cold,
    And the brotherhood of friars;
        Not a name
        Remains to fame,
From those mouldering days of old!

But the poet's memory here
    Of the landscape makes a part;
Like the river, swift and clear,
    Flows his song through many a heart;
        Haunting still
        That ancient mill,
In the Valley of the Vire.

VICTOR GALBRAITH

Under the walls of Monterey
At daybreak the bugles began to play,
    Victor Galbraith!
In the mist of the morning damp and gray,
These were the words they seemed to say:
    "Come forth to thy death,
    Victor Galbraith!"

Forth he came, with a martial tread;
Firm was his step, erect his head;
    Victor Galbraith,
He who so well the bugle played,
Could not mistake the words it said:
    "Come forth to thy death,
    Victor Galbraith!"

He looked at the earth, he looked at the sky,
He looked at the files of musketry,
    Victor Galbraith!
And he said, with a steady voice and eye,
"Take good aim; I am ready to die!"
    Thus challenges death
    Victor Galbraith.

Twelve fiery tongues flashed straight and red,
Six leaden balls on their errand sped;
    Victor Galbraith
Falls to the ground, but he is not dead;
His name was not stamped on those balls of lead,
    And they only scath
    Victor Galbraith.

Three balls are in his breast and brain,
But he rises out of the dust again,
    Victor Galbraith!
The water he drinks has a bloody stain;
"O kill me, and put me out of my pain!"
    In his agony prayeth
    Victor Galbraith.

Forth dart once more those tongues of flame,
And the bugler has died a death of shame,
    Victor Galbraith!
His soul has gone back to whence it came,
And no one answers to the name,
    When the Sergeant saith,
    "Victor Galbraith!"

Under the walls of Monterey
By night a bugle is heard to play,
    Victor Galbraith!
Through the mist of the valley damp and gray
The sentinels hear the sound, and say,
    "That is the wraith
    Of Victor Galbraith!"

MY LOST YOUTH

Often I think of the beautiful town
    That is seated by the sea;
Often in thought go up and down
The pleasant streets of that dear old town,
    And my youth comes back to me.
      And a verse of a Lapland song
      Is haunting my memory still:
    "A boy's will is the wind's will,
And the thoughts of youth are long, long thoughts."

I can see the shadowy lines of its trees,
    And catch, in sudden gleams,
The sheen of the far-surrounding seas,
And islands that were the Hersperides
    Of all my boyish dreams.
      And the burden of that old song,
      It murmurs and whispers still:
    "A boy's will is the wind's will,
And the thoughts of youth are long, long thoughts."

I remember the black wharves and the slips,
    And the sea-tides tossing free;
And Spanish sailors with bearded lips,
And the beauty and mystery of the ships,
    And the magic of the sea.
      And the voice of that wayward song
      Is singing and saying still:
    "A boy's will is the wind's will,
And the thoughts of youth are long, long thoughts."

I remember the bulwarks by the shore,
   And the fort upon the hill;
The sunrise gun, with its hollow roar,
The drum-beat repeated o'er and o'er,
   And the bugle wild and shrill.
      And the music of that old song
      Throbs in my memory still:
"A boy's will is the wind's will,
And the thoughts of youth are long, long thoughts."

I remember the sea-fight far away,
   How it thundered o'er the tide!
And the dead captains, as they lay
In their graves, o'erlooking the tranquil bay,
   Where they in battle died.
      And the sound of that mournful song
      Goes through me with a thrill:
"A boy's will is the wind's will,
And the thoughts of youth are long, long thoughts."

I can see the breezy dome of groves,
   The shadows of Deering's Woods;
And the friendships old and the early loves
Come back with a sabbath sound, as of doves
   In quiet neighborhoods.
      And the verse of that sweet old song,
      It flutters and murmurs still:
"A boy's will is the wind's will,
And the thoughts of youth are long, long thoughts."

I remember the gleams and glooms that dart
   Across the school-boy's brain;
The song and the silence in the heart,
That in part are prophecies, and in part
   Are longings wild and vain.

And the voice of that fitful song
   Sings on, and is never still:
"A boy's will is the wind's will,
And the thoughts of youth are long, long thoughts."

There are things of which I may not speak;
   There are dreams that cannot die;
There are thoughts that make the strong heart weak,
And bring a pallor into the cheek,
   And a mist before the eye.
     And the words of that fatal song
     Come over me like a chill:
"A boy's will is the wind's will,
And the thoughts of youth are long, long thoughts."

Strange to me now are the forms I meet
   When I visit the dear old town;
But the native air is pure and sweet,
And the trees that o'ershadow each well-known street,
   As they balance up and down,
     Are singing the beautiful song,
     Are sighing and whispering still:
"A boy's will is the wind's will,
And the thoughts of youth are long, long thoughts."

And Deering's Woods are fresh and fair,
   And with joy that is almost pain
My heart goes back to wander there,
And among the dreams of the days that were,
   I find my lost youth again.
     And the strange and beautiful song,
     The groves are repeating it still:
"A boy's will is the wind's will,
And the thoughts of youth are long, long thoughts."

THE ROPEWALK

In that building, long and low,
With its windows all a-row,
    Like the port-holes of a hulk,
Human spiders spin and spin,
Backward down their threads so thin
    Dropping, each a hempen bulk.

At the end, an open door;
Squares of sunshine on the floor
    Light the long and dusky lane;
And the whirring of a wheel,
Dull and drowsy, makes me feel
    All its spokes are in my brain.

As the spinners to the end
Downward go and reascend,
    Gleam the long threads in the sun;
While within this brain of mine
Cobwebs brighter and more fine
    By the busy wheel are spun.

Two fair maidens in a swing,
Like white doves upon the wing,
    First before my vision pass;
Laughing, as their gentle hands
Closely clasp the twisted strands,
    At their shadow on the grass.

Then a booth of mountebanks,
With its smell of tan and planks,
   And a girl poised high in air
On a cord, in spangled dress,
With a faded loveliness,
   And a weary look of care.

Then a homestead among farms,
And a woman with bare arms
   Drawing water from a well;
As the bucket mounts apace,
With it mounts her own fair face,
   As at some magician's spell.

Then an old man in a tower,
Ringing loud the noontide hour,
   While the rope coils round and round
Like a serpent at his feet,
And again, in swift retreat,
   Nearly lifts him from the ground.

Then within a prison-yard,
Faces fixed, and stern, and hard,
   Laughter and indecent mirth;
Ah! it is the gallows-tree!
Breath of Christian charity,
   Blow, and sweep it from the earth!

Then a school-boy, with his kite
Gleaming in a sky of light,
   And an eager, upward look;
Steeds pursued through lane and field;
Fowlers with their snares concealed;
   And an angler by a brook.

Ships rejoicing in the breeze,
Wrecks that float o'er unknown seas,
   Anchors dragged through faithless sand;
Sea-fog drifting overhead,
And, with lessening line and lead,
 S ailors feeling for the land.

All these scenes do I behold,
These, and many left untold,
   In that building long and low;
While the wheel goes round and round,
With a drowsy, dreamy sound,
   And the spinners backward go.

THE GOLDEN MILE-STONE

Leafless are the trees; their purple branches
Spread themselves abroad, like reefs of coral,
    Rising silent
In the Red Sea of the winter sunset.

From the hundred chimneys of the village,
Like the Afreet in the Arabian story,
    Smoky columns
Tower aloft into the air of amber.

At the window winks the flickering fire-light;
Here and there the lamps of evening glimmer,
    Social watch-fires
Answering one another through the darkness.

On the hearth the lighted logs are glowing,
And like Ariel in the cloven pine-tree
    For its freedom
Groans and sighs the air imprisoned in them.

By the fireside there are old men seated,
Seeing ruined cities in the ashes,
    Asking sadly
Of the Past what it can ne'er restore them.

By the fireside there are youthful dreamers,
Building castles fair, with stately stairways,
    Asking blindly
Of the Future what it cannot give them.

By the fireside tragedies are acted
In whose scenes appear two actors only,
   Wife and husband,
And above them God the sole spectator.

By the fireside there are peace and comfort,
Wives and children, with fair, thoughtful faces,
   Waiting, watching
For a well-known footstep in the passage.

Each man's chimney is his Golden Mile-Stone;
Is the central point, from which he measures
   Every distance
Through the gateways of the world around him.

In his farthest wanderings still he sees it;
Hears the talking flame, the answering night-wind,
   As he heard them
When he sat with those who were, but are not.

Happy he whom neither wealth nor fashion,
Nor the march of the encroaching city,
   Drives an exile
From the hearth of his ancestral homestead.

We may build more splendid habitations,
Fill our rooms with paintings and with sculptures,
   But we cannot
Buy with gold the old associations!

CATAWBA WINE

This song of mine
  Is a Song of the Vine,
To be sung by the glowing embers
  Of wayside inns,
  When the rain begins
To darken the drear Novembers.

It is not a song
  Of the Scuppernong,
From warm Carolinian valleys,
  Nor the Isabel
  And the Muscadel
That bask in our garden alleys.

Nor the red Mustang,
  Whose clusters hang
O'er the waves of the Colorado,
  And the fiery flood
  Of whose purple blood
Has a dash of Spanish bravado.

For richest and best
  Is the wine of the West,
That grows by the Beautiful River;
  Whose sweet perfume
  Fills all the room
With a benison on the giver.

And as hollow trees
Are the haunts of bees,
Forever going and coming;
So this crystal hive
Is all alive
With a swarming and buzzing and humming.

Very good in its way
Is the Verzenay,
Or the Sillery soft and creamy;
But Catawba wine
Has a taste more divine,
More dulcet, delicious, and dreamy.

There grows no vine
By the haunted Rhine,
By Danube or Guadalquivir,
Nor on island or cape,
That bears such a grape
As grows by the Beautiful River.

Drugged is their juice
For foreign use,
When shipped o'er the reeling Atlantic,
To rack our brains
With the fever pains,
That have driven the Old World frantic.

To the sewers and sinks
With all such drinks,
And after them tumble the mixer;
For a poison malign
Is such Borgia wine,
Or at best but a Devil's Elixir.

While pure as a spring
Is the wine I sing,
And to praise it, one needs but name it;
For Catawba wine
Has need of no sign,
No tavern-bush to proclaim it.

And this Song of the Vine,
This greeting of mine,
The winds and the birds shall deliver
To the Queen of the West,
In her garlands dressed,
On the banks of the Beautiful River.

SANTA FILOMENA

Whene'er a noble deed is wrought,
Whene'er is spoken a noble thought,
    Our hearts, in glad surprise,
    To higher levels rise.

The tidal wave of deeper souls
Into our inmost being rolls,
    And lifts us unawares
    Out of all meaner cares.

Honor to those whose words or deeds
Thus help us in our daily needs,
    And by their overflow
    Raise us from what is low!

Thus thought I, as by night I read
Of the great army of the dead,
    The trenches cold and damp,
    The starved and frozen camp,--

The wounded from the battle-plain,
In dreary hospitals of pain,
    The cheerless corridors,
    The cold and stony floors.

Lo! in that house of misery
A lady with a lamp I see
    Pass through the glimmering gloom,
    And flit from room to room.

And slow, as in a dream of bliss,
The speechless sufferer turns to kiss
    Her shadow, as it falls
    Upon the darkening walls.

As if a door in heaven should be
Opened and then closed suddenly,
    The vision came and went,
    The light shone and was spent.

On England's annals, through the long
Hereafter of her speech and song,
    That light its rays shall cast
    From portals of the past.

A Lady with a Lamp shall stand
In the great history of the land,
    A noble type of good,
    Heroic womanhood.

Nor even shall be wanting here
The palm, the lily, and the spear,
    The symbols that of yore
    Saint Filomena bore.

THE DISCOVERER OF THE NORTH CAPE

A Leaf from King Alfred's Orosius

Othere, the old sea-captain,
    Who dwelt in Helgoland,
To King Alfred, the Lover of Truth,
Brought a snow-white walrus-tooth,
    Which he held in his brown right hand.

His figure was tall and stately,
    Like a boy's his eye appeared;
His hair was yellow as hay,
But threads of a silvery gray
    Gleamed in his tawny beard.

Hearty and hale was Othere,
    His cheek had the color of oak;
With a kind of laugh in his speech,
Like the sea-tide on a beach,
    As unto the King he spoke.

And Alfred, King of the Saxons,
    Had a book upon his knees,
And wrote down the wondrous tale
Of him who was first to sail
    Into the Arctic seas.

"So far I live to the northward,
    No man lives north of me;
To the east are wild mountain-chains;
And beyond them meres and plains;
    To the westward all is sea.

"So far I live to the northward,
   From the harbor of Skeringes-hale,
If you only sailed by day,
With a fair wind all the way,
   More than a month would you sail.

"I own six hundred reindeer,
   With sheep and swine beside;
I have tribute from the Finns,
Whalebone and reindeer-skins,
   And ropes of walrus-hide.

"I ploughed the land with horses,
   But my heart was ill at ease,
For the old seafaring men
Came to me now and then,
   With their sagas of the seas;--

"Of Iceland and of Greenland,
   And the stormy Hebrides,
And the undiscovered deep;--
Oh I could not eat nor sleep
   For thinking of those seas.

"To the northward stretched the desert,
   How far I fain would know;
So at last I sallied forth,
And three days sailed due north,
   As far as the whale-ships go.

"To the west of me was the ocean,
   To the right the desolate shore,
But I did not slacken sail
For the walrus or the whale,
   Till after three days more.

"The days grew longer and longer,
    Till they became as one,
And northward through the haze
I saw the sullen blaze
    Of the red midnight sun.

"And then uprose before me,
    Upon the water's edge,
The huge and haggard shape
Of that unknown North Cape,
    Whose form is like a wedge.

"The sea was rough and stormy,
    The tempest howled and wailed,
And the sea-fog, like a ghost,
Haunted that dreary coast,
    But onward still I sailed.

"Four days I steered to eastward,
    Four days without a night:
Round in a fiery ring
Went the great sun, O King,
    With red and lurid light."

Here Alfred, King of the Saxons,
    Ceased writing for a while;
And raised his eyes from his book,
With a strange and puzzled look,
    And an incredulous smile.

But Othere, the old sea-captain,
    He neither paused nor stirred,
Till the King listened, and then
Once more took up his pen,
    And wrote down every word.

"And now the land," said Othere,
  "Bent southward suddenly,
And I followed the curving shore
And ever southward bore
  Into a nameless sea.

"And there we hunted the walrus,
  The narwhale, and the seal;
Ha! 't was a noble game!
And like the lightning's flame
  Flew our harpoons of steel.

"There were six of us all together,
  Norsemen of Helgoland;
In two days and no more
We killed of them threescore,
  And dragged them to the strand!"

Here Alfred the Truth-Teller
  Suddenly closed his book,
And lifted his blue eyes,
With doubt and strange surmise
  Depicted in their look.

And Othere the old sea-captain
  Stared at him wild and weird,
Then smiled, till his shining teeth
Gleamed white from underneath
  His tawny, quivering beard.

And to the King of the Saxons,
  In witness of the truth,
Raising his noble head,
He stretched his brown hand, and said,
  "Behold this walrus-tooth!"

DAYBREAK

A wind came up out of the sea,
And said, "O mists, make room for me."

It hailed the ships, and cried, "Sail on,
Ye mariners, the night is gone."

And hurried landward far away,
Crying, "Awake! it is the day."

It said unto the forest, "Shout!
Hang all your leafy banners out!"

It touched the wood-bird's folded wing,
And said, "O bird, awake and sing."

And o'er the farms, "O chanticleer,
Your clarion blow; the day is near."

It whispered to the fields of corn,
"Bow down, and hail the coming morn."

It shouted through the belfry-tower,
"Awake, O bell! proclaim the hour."

It crossed the churchyard with a sigh,
And said, "Not yet! in quiet lie."

THE FIFTIETH BIRTHDAY OF AGASSIZ

May 28, 1857

It was fifty years ago
    In the pleasant month of May,
In the beautiful Pays de Vaud,
    A child in its cradle lay.

And Nature, the old nurse, took
    The child upon her knee,
Saying: "Here is a story-book
    Thy Father has written for thee."

"Come, wander with me," she said,
    "Into regions yet untrod;
And read what is still unread
    In the manuscripts of God."

And he wandered away and away
    With Nature, the dear old nurse,
Who sang to him night and day
    The rhymes of the universe.

And whenever the way seemed long,
    Or his heart began to fail,
She would sing a more wonderful song,
    Or tell a more marvellous tale.

So she keeps him still a child,
    And will not let him go,
Though at times his heart beats wild
    For the beautiful Pays de Vaud;

Though at times he hears in his dreams
    The Ranz des Vaches of old,
And the rush of mountain streams
    From glaciers clear and cold;

And the mother at home says, "Hark!
    For his voice I listen and yearn;
It is growing late and dark,
    And my boy does not return!"

May 28, 1857

CHILDREN

Come to me, O ye children!
   For I hear you at your play,
And the questions that perplexed me
   Have vanished quite away.

Ye open the eastern windows,
   That look towards the sun,
Where thoughts are singing swallows
   And the brooks of morning run.

In your hearts are the birds and the sunshine,
   In your thoughts the brooklet's flow,
But in mine is the wind of Autumn
   And the first fall of the snow.

Ah! what would the world be to us
   If the children were no more?
We should dread the desert behind us
   Worse than the dark before.

What the leaves are to the forest,
   With light and air for food,
Ere their sweet and tender juices
   Have been hardened into wood,—

That to the world are children;
   Through them it feels the glow
Of a brighter and sunnier climate
   Than reaches the trunks below.

Come to me, O ye children!
    And whisper in my ear
What the birds and the winds are singing
    In your sunny atmosphere.

For what are all our contrivings,
    And the wisdom of our books,
When compared with your caresses,
    And the gladness of your looks?

Ye are better than all the ballads
    That ever were sung or said;
For ye are living poems,
    And all the rest are dead.

SANDALPHON

Have you read in the Talmud of old,
In the Legends the Rabbins have told
    Of the limitless realms of the air,--
Have you read it,--the marvellous story
Of Sandalphon, the Angel of Glory,
    Sandalphon, the Angel of Prayer?

How, erect, at the outermost gates
Of the City Celestial he waits,
    With his feet on the ladder of light,
That, crowded with angels unnumbered,
By Jacob was seen, as he slumbered
    Alone in the desert at night?

The Angels of Wind and of Fire
Chant only one hymn, and expire
    With the song's irresistible stress;
Expire in their rapture and wonder,
As harp-strings are broken asunder
    By music they throb to express.

But serene in the rapturous throng,
Unmoved by the rush of the song,
    With eyes unimpassioned and slow,
Among the dead angels, the deathless
Sandalphon stands listening breathless
    To sounds that ascend from below;--

From the spirits on earth that adore,
From the souls that entreat and implore
    In the fervor and passion of prayer;
From the hearts that are broken with losses,
And weary with dragging the crosses
    Too heavy for mortals to bear.

And he gathers the prayers as he stands,
And they change into flowers in his hands,
    Into garlands of purple and red;
And beneath the great arch of the portal,
Through the streets of the City Immortal
    Is wafted the fragrance they shed.

It is but a legend, I know,--
A fable, a phantom, a show,
    Of the ancient Rabbinical lore;
Yet the old mediaeval tradition,
The beautiful, strange superstition,
    But haunts me and holds me the more.

When I look from my window at night,
And the welkin above is all white,
    All throbbing and panting with stars,
Among them majestic is standing
Sandalphon the angel, expanding
    His pinions in nebulous bars.

And the legend, I feel, is a part
Of the hunger and thirst of the heart,
    The frenzy and fire of the brain,
That grasps at the fruitage forbidden,
The golden pomegranates of Eden,
    To quiet its fever and pain.

EPIMETHEUS,
OR THE POET'S AFTERTHOUGHT

Have I dreamed? or was it real,
    What I saw as in a vision,
When to marches hymeneal
In the land of the Ideal
    Moved my thought o'er Fields Elysian?

What! are these the guests whose glances
    Seemed like sunshine gleaming round me?
These the wild, bewildering fancies,
That with dithyrambic dances
    As with magic circles bound me?

Ah! how cold are their caresses!
    Pallid cheeks, and haggard bosoms!
Spectral gleam their snow-white dresses,
And from loose, dishevelled tresses
    Fall the hyacinthine blossoms!

O my songs! whose winsome measures
    Filled my heart with secret rapture!
Children of my golden leisures!
Must even your delights and pleasures
    Fade and perish with the capture?

Fair they seemed, those songs sonorous,
    When they came to me unbidden;
Voices single, and in chorus,
Like the wild birds singing o'er us
    In the dark of branches hidden.

Disenchantment! Disillusion!
 Must each noble aspiration
Come at last to this conclusion,
Jarring discord, wild confusion,
 Lassitude, renunciation?

Not with steeper fall nor faster,
 From the sun's serene dominions,
Not through brighter realms nor vaster,
In swift ruin and disaster,
 Icarus fell with shattered pinions!

Sweet Pandora! dear Pandora!
 Why did mighty Jove create thee
Coy as Thetis, fair as Flora,
Beautiful as young Aurora,
 If to win thee is to hate thee?

No, not hate thee! for this feeling
 Of unrest and long resistance
Is but passionate appealing,
A prophetic whisper stealing
 O'er the chords of our existence.

Him whom thou dost once enamour,
 Thou, beloved, never leavest;
In life's discord, strife, and clamor,
Still he feels thy spell of glamour;
 Him of Hope thou ne'er bereavest.

Weary hearts by thee are lifted,
 Struggling souls by thee are strengthened,
Clouds of fear asunder rifted,
Truth from falsehood cleansed and sifted,
 Lives, like days in summer, lengthened!

Therefore art thou ever dearer,
   O my Sibyl, my deceiver!
For thou makest each mystery clearer,
And the unattained seems nearer,
   When thou fillest my heart with fever!

Muse of all the Gifts and Graces!
   Though the fields around us wither,
There are ampler realms and spaces,
Where no foot has left its traces:
   Let us turn and wander thither!

NOTES

The Ladder of St. Augustine — p. 73

That of our vices we can frame
A ladder.

The words of St. Augustine are, " De vitiis nostris scalam nobis facimus, si vitia ipsa calcamus."

Sermon III. *De Ascensione.*

The Phantom Ship — p. 75

A detailed account of this "apparition of a Ship in the Air" is given by Cotton Mather in his Magnalia Christi, Book I. Ch. VI. It is contained in a letter from the Rev. James Pierpont, Pastor of New Haven. To this account Mather adds these words :

"Reader, there being yet living so many credible gentlemen, that were eyewitnesses of this wonderful thing, I venture to publish it for a thing as undoubted as 't is wonderful."

The Emperor's Bird's-Nest — p. 83

And the Emperor but a Macho.

Macho, in Spanish, signifies a mule. *Golondrina* is the feminine form of *Golondrino*, a swallow, and also a cant name for a deserter.

Oliver Basselin — p. 93

Oliver Basselin, the *"Père joyeux du Vaudeville,"* flourished in the fifteenth century, and gave to his convivial songs the name of his native valleys, in which he sang them, Vaux-de-Vire. This name was afterwards corrupted into the modern Vaudeville.

Victor Galbraith — p. 97

This poem is founded on fact. Victor Galbraith was a bugler in a company of volunteer cavalry; and was shot in Mexico for some breach of discipline. It is a common superstition among soldiers, that no balls will kill them unless their names are written on them. The old proverb says, "Every bullet has its billet."

My Lost Youth — p. 99

I remember the sea-fight far away.

This was the engagement between the Enterprise and Boxer, off the harbor of Portland, in which both captains were slain. They were buried side by side, in the cemetery on Mountjoy.

Santa Filomena — p. 113

"At Pisa the church of San Francisco contains a chapel dedicated lately to Santa Filomena ; over the altar is a picture, by Sabatelli, representing the Saint as a beautiful, nymph-like figure, floating down from heaven, attended by two angels bearing the lily, palm, and javelin, and beneath, in the foreground, the sick and maimed, who are healed by her intercession." —Mrs. JAMESON, *Sacred and Legendary Art,* II. 298.

ABOUT THE AUTHOR

Henry Wadsworth Longfellow (1807-1882) was an American poet and educator. His best-known original works include "Paul Revere's Ride," "The Song of Hiawatha" and "Evangeline." He was the first American to completely translate Dante Alighieri's "Divine Comedy" and was one of the fireside poets from New England.

Longfellow wrote many lyric poems known for their musicality and often presenting stories of mythology and legend. He became the most popular American poet of his day and had success overseas. He has been criticized for imitating European styles and writing poetry that was too sentimental.

1807

—February 27, 1807: Birth of Henry Wadsworth Longfellow at Portland, Maine (which was at that time still part of Massachusetts). He was the son of Stephen Longfellow, a lawyer, and Zilch Wadsworth, daughter of Peleg Wadsworth, a general in the American Revolutionary War and a member of Congress. His mother was descended from Richard Warren, who was a passenger on the Mayflower. His Mayflower ancestors also included William Brewster and John and Priscilla Alden.

1810
—Longfellow att4ends a dame school at age three.
1812
—April 30: Louisiana becomes the 18th state to j
—June 18: The War of 1812 begins, during which the United States of America and its indigenous allies fought against the United Kingdom and its allies in British North America.

1813
—Longfellow is enrolled at age six at the private Portland Academy.
—A naval battle occurs between American and British sips offshore of New England. The treaty restored diplomatic relations and restored the pre-war borders of June 1812.

1814
—December 24: The Treaty of Ghent, a peace treaty concluding the War of 1812, was signed at Ghent, in the Netherlands, by representatives of the United States and the United Kingdom.

1816
—The statehood of Indiana is recognized, and Indiana becomes the 19th state of the Union. Indiana had previously been part of the Northwest Territory organized in 1787.

1817
—December 10: Mississippi becomes the 20th state admitted to the Union of the United States. Mississippi seceded from the Union and was restored to the Union in 1870, after the American Civil War.

1818
—Illinois achieved statehood after being part of the Northwest

Territory for many years, becoming the 21st state of the Union.

1819

—December The statehood of Alabama is recognized. Alabama would later secede from the Union in 1861, rejoining the Union in 1868 after the American Civil War.

1820

—March 15: Maine becomes the 23rd state of the United States, as part of the Missouri Compromise, after residents voted to secede from the Commonwealth of Massachusetts.
—Longfellow's first poem, "The Battle of Lovell's Pond," was published in the Portland Gazette on November 17, 1820. It was a patriotic and historical four-stanza poem.
—Nathaniel Hawthorne enrolls at Bowdoin College.

1821

—The former Missouri Territory is admitted to the Union as a slave state as part of the Missouri Compromise. Although the Confederacy recognized Missouri as its twelfth state, the secession was disputed and later regarded as not in effect.

1822

—Longfellow enrolls at Bowdoin College in Brunswick, Maine, along with his brother Stephen. His grandfather was a founder of the college and his father was a trustee. Here he met Nathaniel Hawthorne, a lifelong friend.

1824

—Nearly 40 minor poems by Longfellow are published between January 1824 and his graduation in 1825, many of these at the short-lived Boston periodical, The United States Literary Gazette."

1825

—Longfellow graduates from Bowdoin College, fourth in his class and elected to Phi Beta Kappa. He gave the student commencement address.

—Longfellow is offered a job as professor of modern languages at his alma mater, on condition that he prepare by touring Europe and learning Romance languages.

1826

—January 30: Washington Irving, while living in Paris, is invited to travel to Madrid to inspect the Spanish archives in the library of the American consul.

—In May, Longfellow travels from New York to Le Havre, in France, aboard the ship 'Cadmus.' He spent three years in Europe, visiting France, Spain, Italy, Germany, and England. During his time abroad he learned French, Italian, Spanish, Portuguese, and German, mostly without formal instruction. While in Madrid, he met with Washington Irving, who encouraged his writing.

—July 4: Former U.S. Presidents Thomas Jefferson and John Adams both die on the 50th anniversary of the signing of the United States Declaration of Independence.

1827

—In the United Kingdom, George Canning succeeds Lord Liverpool as British prime minister.

—The term "socialist" is coined by Robert Owen in his London periodical, The Co-operative Magazine and Monthly Herald.

1828

—January: Washington Irving's book, "A History of the Life and Voyages of Christopher Columbus," was published.

—The first substantial praise of Longfellow's work is published, by John Neal, a fellow native of Portland, Maine, in the January 23, 1828 issue of his magazine, "The Yankee." He wrote: "As for Mr. Longfellow, he has a fine genius and a pure and safe taste,..."

—December 3: Andrew Jackson is elected President of the United States, defeating incumbent John Quincy Adams.

1829

—March 22; Greece receives autonomy from the Ottoman Empire.

—July 23: In the United States, William Burt obtains the first patent for a form of typewriter, the typographer.

—In mid-August, Longfellow returns to the United States.

—August 27: Longfellow wrote to the president of Bowdoin that he was turning down the professorship because he considered the $600 salary "disproportionate to the duties required." The trustees raised his salary to $800 with an additional $100 to serve as the college's librarian, which required one hour of work per day. While teaching at the college he translated textbooks from French, Italian, and Spanish.

1831

—July 21: Leopold of Saxe-Coburg-Gotha is inaugurated as the first King of the Belgians in Brussels.

—September 14, Longfellow marries Mary Storer, a childhood friend from Portland, Maine.

1832

—February 28: Charles Darwin and the crew of HMS Beagle arrive at South America for the first time.

—Greece is recognized as a sovereign nation by the Treaty of Constantinople, ending the Greek War of Independence.

1833

—Washington Irving's book, "Tales of the Alhambra," a book of short stories, is published.

—Longfellow's first published book was a translation of poetry by the medieval Spanish poet, Jorge Manrique, "Coplas de Don Jorge Manrique."

—Publication of several nonfiction and fiction prose pieces inspired by Irving, including "The Indian Summer" and "The Bald Eagle."

1834

—Longfellow receives a letter from Harvard College offering him the Smith Professorship of Modern Languages, with the stipulation that he spend a year abroad. He and his wife travel to Europe, where he studies German as well as Dutch, Danish, Swedish, Finnish, and Icelandic.

—The Spanish Inquisition, which had begun in the 15th century, is suppressed by royal decree.

1835

—Publication of "Outer-Mer: A Pilgrimage Beyond the Sea," a collection of Prose works by Longfellow. The term "outer-mer" is French for "overseas."

—September 7: Charles Darwin arrives at the Galapagos Islands, aboard HMS Beagle.

—November 29: Death of Longfellow's first wife, after a miscarriage. Her body was shipped home to the United States for burial at Mount Auburn Cemetery near Boston.

—December 28: The Second Seminole War led by Osceola breaks out.

1836

—Longfellow returns to the United States and assumes the professorship at Harvard.

—June 15: Arkansas is the 25th state admitted into the United States of America. Arkansas seceded from the Union in 1861 and rejoined in 186, after the American Civil War.

—Sam Houston is elected as the first president of the Republic of Texas.

1837

—January 26: Michigan becomes the 26th state of the United States, following the Toledo War, a boundary dispute with Ohio, in which Ohio was granted the Toledo region and Michigan was given the western part of the Upper Peninsula.

—During the spring Longfellow has rented rooms at the Craigie House, built in 1759, which served as the headquarters of George Washington during the Siege of Boston. Previous boarders included Jared Sparks, Edward Everett, and Joseph Emerson Worcester. The house is preserved as the Longfellow House-Washington's Headquarters National Historic Site.

—Charles Dickens's "Oliver Twist" begins publication in serial form in London.

1838

—Longfellow writes the poem, "Footsteps of Angels," said to be about his late wife.

—June 28: The coronation of Queen Victoria takes place at Westminster Abbey in London.

—July 4: The Iowa Territory is formally established after a bill signed by U.S. President Martin Van Buren on June 12.

1839

—Publication of Longfellow's first poetry collection, "Voices of the Night," his first book of poetry. Although most of the book was translations, it included nine original poems and seven poems that he had written as a teenager.

—During Longfellow's seven-year long courtship of Frances "Fanny" Appleton, whose family lived at Beacon Hill in Boston. He often walked from Cambridge to the Appleton home by crossing the Boston Bridge. That bridge was replaced in 1906 with a new bridge later renamed as the Longfellow Bridge.

—Publication of "Hyperion: A Romance," a romance novel, whose

HENRY WADSWORTH LONGFELLOW

main character, Paul Flemming, travels through Germany and falls in love with an Englishwoman who rejects him. The semi-autobiographical novel hints of his own travels, his atheistic beliefs and his own as yet unsuccessful courtship. The novel's descriptions of Germany would later inspire its use as a companion travel guide for American tourists in that country.

1840?

—Longfellow takes a six-month leave of absence from Harvard to attend a health spa in the former Marienberg Benedictine Convent at Boppard in Germany

1841

—Publication of Longfellow's "Ballads and Other Poems," which included "The Village Blacksmith" and "The Wreck of the Hesperus."
—January 26: Britain occupies Hong Kong, an island with a population of 7,500.
—March 4: William Henry Harrison is sworn in as the ninth President of the United States.
—April 6: John Tyler is sworn in as the tenth President of the United States, two days after Harrison's death of pneumonia.

1842

—Publication of the drama "The Spanish Student: A Play in Three Acts," a play in which he reflects on his time in Spain in the 1820s.
—Publication of Longfellow's "Poems on Slavery," his first public support of abolitionism and anti-slavery efforts. Most of the poems were written at sea in October 1842. The poems were later reprinted as anti-slavery tracts in 1843, and included: "To William E. Channing," "The Slave's Dream," "The Good Part," "The Slave in the Dismal Swamp," "The Slave

Singing at Midnight," "The Witnesses," "The Quadroon Girl," and "The Warning."

1843

—Longfellow marries Frances Elizabeth Appleton.

—Nathan Appleton, the father of Longfellow's wife, purchases the former Craigie house as a wedding present, and Longfellow lives there for the rest of his life.

1844

—Birth of Charles Appleton Longfellow

—Publication of "Poets and Poetry of Europe," with translations by Longfellow.

1845

—March 3: Florida is admitted to the Union as the 27th state. Florida, an area previously contested by Spain and Great Britain, had been ceded to the United States in 1819. Florida seceded from the Union in 1861 and rejoined in 1868, after the American Civil War.

—March 4: James K. Polk (1795-1849) is sworn in as the 11th president of the United States of America.

—Birth of Ernest Wadsworth Longfellow

—Publication of "The Belfry of Bruges and Other Poems," a poetry collection.

—Publication of "The Waif: A Collection of Poems," an anthology of poems by various authors, to which Longfellow contributed "Proem."

—December 29: Texas is recognized as the 28th state of the United States.

1846

—December 28, 1846: Iowa becomes the 29th state in the Union.

1847

—April 7: Birth of Fanny Longfellow, the Longfellows' first daughter. During childbirth, Dr. Nathan Cooley Keep administered ether to the mother as the first obstetric anesthetic in the United States.

—November 1: Publication of Longfellow's epic poem, "Evangeline: A Tale of Acadia."

1848

—May 29: Wisconsin becomes the 30th state to join the United States.

1849

—Publication of "Kavanagh: A Tale," a story of a country romance, in which Mr. Churchill, a school teacher, who has always planned to write a romance, but whose procrastination has never allowed him to start, until late in life he resigns himself to his "destiny."

—March 4: Major General Zachary Taylor (1784-1850) is sworn in as the 12th president of the United States of America.

1850

—Birth of Alice Mary Longfellow

—Publication of "The Seaside and the Fireside," a poetry collection.

—March 4: Millard Fillmore (1800-1874) is sworn in as the 13th president of the United States.

1851

—Publication of "The Golden Legend," a poem.

1852

—Publication of "The Poetical Works of Henry Wadsworth Longfellow," a poetry collection, in London, with illustrations by John Gilbert.

1853

—Birth of Edith Longfellow

—March 4: Franklin Pierce (1804-1869) is sworn in as the 14th president of the United States of America.

—June 13: Longfellow hosts a farewell dinner party at his Cambridge home for his friend Nathaniel Hawthorne, who was preparing to move overseas.

1854

—Longfellow retired from his teaching position at Harvard to focus on his writing

1855

—Birth of Anne Allegra Longfellow

—Publication of "The Song of Hiawatha," an epic poem in trochaic tetrameter, featuring Native American characters. The epic tells the fictional adventures of an Ojibwe warrior named Hiawatha and the tragedy of his love for Minnehaha, a Dakota woman.

1857

—March 4: James Buchanan (1791-1868) is sworn in as the 15th president of the United States of America.

1858

—May 11: The Minnesota Territory is admitted to the Union as the 32nd state in the United States.

—Publication of "The Courtship of Miles Standish and Other Poems," a poetry collection. "The Courtship of Miles Standish" is a narrative poem, written in dactylic hexameter, about the early days of Plymouth Colony, the colonial settlement established in America by the Mayflower pilgrims. The poem was among the most enduringly popular of Longfellow's works.

1859

—February 14: Oregon is admitted to the Union as the 33rd state of the United States.

—Longfellow is awarded an honorary doctorate of laws from Harvard.

1860

—April 6: Longfellow writes the poem, "Paul Revere's Ride," commemorating the actions of Paul Revere on April 18, 1775, when he was said to warn American patriot defenders of the approaching British, although not a historically accurate account. It was written the day after Longfellow visited the Old North Church in Boston and climbed its tower It was first published in the January 1861 issue of 'The Atlantic Monthly.' Longfellow's family was said to have a connection to the historical Paul Revere in that his maternal grandfather, Peleg Wadsworth, had been Revere's commander during the Penobscot Expedition.

1861

—January 29: Kansas becomes the 39th state to join the United States.

—March 4: Abraham Lincoln (1809-1865) is sworn in as the 16th president of the United States of America.

—April 12: Start of the American Civil War, in which the Union states and the states of the southern Confederacy fought over issues of slavery.

—July 9: Longfellow's wife was sealing an envelope with hot sealing wax, or lighting a match, when her dress caught fire and her body was badly burned.

—July 10: Death of Francis Appleton, Longfellow's wife.

—Death of Longfellow's second wife, after sustaining burns when her dress caught fire. The distraught Longfellow was himself was injured by burns on his face, after trying to quench the flames with his body, and after that wore a beard to conceal the scars.

1863

—January 1: The Emancipation Proclamation was a presidential proclamation and executive order issued by Abraham Lincoln granted freedom to the slaves of the Confederacy.
—June 20: West Virginia is admitted to the Union as the 35th state of the United States, after seceding from the Confederate State of Virginia.
—July 1-3: The Battle of Gettysburg, fought near the town of Gettysburg in Pennsylvania, in which Union forces halted the Confederates' invasion to the north, was considered a turning point of the American Civil War.
—Publication of "The Legend of Rabbi Ben Levi," a poem telling about Yehoshua ben Levi, a Jewish rabbi and scholar of the Talmud who lived in the land of Israel in the first half of the third century, and taught in the city of Lod, and was known for his debates of theological matters.
—November 23: Publication of "Tales of a Wayside Inn," a poetry collection, in which a group of people gathered at the Wayside Inn in Sudbury, Massachusetts, (about 20 miles from the poet's home in Cambridge), each take turns each telling a story in a variety of poetic forms and styles. The characters are said to be loosely based on actual persons of Longfellow's acquaintance. Includes his previously published poem, "Paul Revere's Ride," and "The Saga of King Olaf." Includes the "second flight" of "Birds of Passage").
—December 25: Longfellow writes the poem "Christmas Bells," which becomes the lyrics of the beloved Christmas carol, "I Heard the Bells on Christmas Day."

1864

—Longfellow launches the "Dante Club," of friends who meet weekly to help with perfecting the translation of Dante Alighieri's "Divine Comedy." Guests included regulars

William Dean Howells, James Russell Lowell, and Charles Eliot Norton.

—October 31: Nevada becomes the 36th state of the Union.

1865

—Longfellow's poem, "Christmas Bells," is published in "Our Young Folks," a juvenile magazine published by Ticknor and Fields.

—Publication of "Household Poems," a poetry collection.

—April 9: Confederate General Robert E. Lee surrenders to Union General Ulysses S. Grant after the Battle of Appomattox Court House.

—April 15: Andrew Johnson (1808-1875) is sworn in as the 17th president of the United States of America, following the assassination of Abraham Lincoln.

1867

—March 1: Nebraska becomes the 37th state of the Union.

—Publication of "The Divine Comedy," Longfellow's translation of Dante Alighieri's work, in three volumes, although revisions continued and the work went through four printings in the first year.

—Publication of "Flower-de-Luce," a poetry collection.

1868

—Publication of "The New England Tragedies," containing two dramatic plays in verse reflecting on events in the early days of New England. The play "John Endicott" dramatizes the clash between the Puritans and the Quakers and the play "Giles Corey of the Salem Farms" is about the Salem witchcraft trials.

1869

—March 4: General Ulysses S. Grant (1822-1885) is sworn in as the 18th president of the United States of America.

1871

—Publication of Longfellow's translation of Dante Alighieri's "The Divine Tragedy," in three volumes.

1872

—Publication of "Christus: A Mystery," a trilogy composed of three previous works: "The Golden Legend," The New England Tragedies," and "The Divine Tragedy."

—Publication of "Three Books of Song," a poetry collection (including the second part of "Tales of a Wayside Inn").

—Longfellow's poem, "Christmas Bells," is set to music by the English organist, John Baptiste Calkin, using a melody called "Waltham." Other melodies have been used, including the 1845 melody of "Mainzer" and a 1956 tune by Johnny Marks, which was popularized by a Bing Crosby recording.

1873

—Publication of "Aftermath," (comprising the third part of "Tales of a Wayside Inn," and the "third flight" of "Birds of Passage").

1874

—Samuel Ward helped Longfellow with the selling of a poem, "The Hanging of the Crane," to the 'New York Ledger' for $3,000, the highest price ever paid for a poem.

—Longfellow oversees the publication of a 31-volume anthology, called "Poems of Places," which collected poems representing geographical locations, including European, Asian, and Arabian countries.

1875

—Publication of "The Masque of Pandora and Other Poems," a poetry collection.

1876

—August 1: Colorado is admitted to the Union, after being organized as the Territory of Colorado since 1861.

1877

—March 4: Rutherford B. Hayes (1822-1893) is sworn in as the 19th president of the United States of America.

1878

—Publication of "Kêramos and Other Poems," a poetry collection.

1880

—Publication of "Ultima Thule," a poetry collection.

1881

—March 4: James A. Garfield ((1831-1881) is sworn in as the 20th president of the United States of America.

1882

—March 24: Death of Longfellow at his home in Cambridge, surrounded by family. He is buried at Mount Auburn Cemetery in Cambridge, Massachusetts.
—Publication of "In the Harbor," a poetry collection.

—Publication of "Michael Angelo: A Fragment," (incomplete, published posthumously).